Microsoft® Office®
Access 2003

Shelley O'Hara

que®

**800 East 96th Street,
Indianapolis, Indiana 46240**

Contents

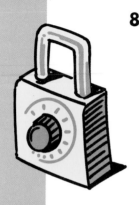

Easy Microsoft® Office® Access 2003

Copyright © 2004 by Que Publishing

International Standard Book Number: 0-7897-2959-8

Library of Congress Catalog Card Number: 2003103656

Printed in the United States of America

First Printing: September 2003

06   05   04   03   4   3   2   1

Bulk Sales

Que Publishing offers excellent discounts on this book when ordered in quantity for bulk purchases or special sales. For more information, please contact

U.S. Corporate and Government Sales
1-800-382-3419
corpsales@pearsontechgroup.com

For sales outside the U.S., please contact

International Sales
1-317-581-3793
international@pearsontechgroup.com

Trademarks

All terms mentioned in this book that are known to be trademarks or service marks have been appropriately capitalized. Que Publishing cannot attest to the accuracy of this information. Use of a term in this book should not be regarded as affecting the validity of any trademark or service mark.

Warning and Disclaimer

Every effort has been made to make this book as complete and as accurate as possible, but no warranty or fitness is implied. The information provided is on an "as is" basis.

Associate Publisher
Greg Wiegand

Acquisitions Editor
Stephanie J. McComb

Development Editor
Kate Shoup Welsh

Managing Editor
Charlotte Clapp

Project Editor
George E. Nedeff

Copy Editor
Geneil Breeze

Indexer
Lisa Wilson

Proofreader
Tracy Donhardt

Technical Editor
Mark Hall

Team Coordinator
Sharry Gregory

Multimedia Developer
Dan Scherf

Interior Designer
Jean Bisesi

Cover Designer
Anne Jones

Page Layout
Brad Chinn

About the Author

Shelley O'Hara is the author of more than 100 books, including several best-sellers. She has also authored business plans, a novel, Web content, marketing publications, short stories, training materials, magazine columns, a newsletter, and software manuals. She has written on topics ranging from Microsoft Windows to the International Air Transport Authority ticketing system, from Microsoft Office to buying a home. In addition to writing, O'Hara teaches training and personal development classes in Indianapolis.

Dedication

To James B. McDaniel, Betty McDaniel Zich, and Vern McDaniel

Acknowledgments

Lucky me! On this project I was again fortunate to work with my favorite team of publishers and editors including Greg Wiegand, Associate Publisher; Stephanie McComb, Acquisitions Editor; Sharry L. Gregory, Team Coordinator; Kate S. Welsh, Development Editor; George Nedeff, Prodject Editor; Geneil Breeze, Copy Editor; and last but certainly not least, Mark Hall, Technical Editor. Y'all are the best.

We Want to Hear from You!

As the reader of this book, *you* are our most important critic and commentator. We value your opinion and want to know what we're doing right, what we could do better, what areas you'd like to see us publish in, and any other words of wisdom you're willing to pass our way.

As an associate publisher for Que Publishing, I welcome your comments. You can email or write me directly to let me know what you did or didn't like about this book—as well as what we can do to make our books better.

Please note that I cannot help you with technical problems related to the *topic* of this book. We do have a User Services group, however, where I will forward specific technical questions related to the book.

When you write, please be sure to include this book's title and author as well as your name, email address, and phone number. I will carefully review your comments and share them with the author and editors who worked on the book.

Email: feedback@quepublishing.com

Mail: Greg Wiegand
          Associate Publisher
          Que Publishing
          800 East 96th Street
          Indianapolis, IN 46240 USA

For more information about this book or another Que Publishing title, visit our Web site at www.quepublishing.com. Type the ISBN (excluding hyphens) or the title of a book in the Search field to find the page you're looking for.

① Each step is fully illustrated to show you how it looks onscreen.

It's as Easy as 1-2-3

Each part of this book is made up of a series of short, instructional lessons, designed to help you understand basic information that you need to get the most out of your computer hardware and software.

② Each task includes a series of quick, easy steps designed to guide you through the procedure.

③ Items that you select or click in menus, dialog boxes, tabs, and windows are shown in **bold**.

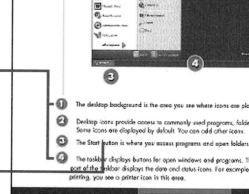
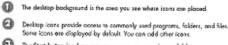

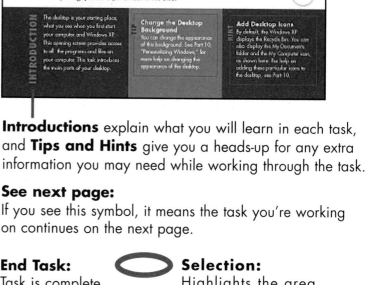

Task 1: Understanding the Desktop

① The desktop background is the area you see where icons are placed.

② Desktop icons provide access to commonly used programs, folders, and files. Some icons are displayed by default. You can add other icons.

③ The Start button is where you access programs and open folders.

④ The taskbar displays buttons for open windows and programs. The status bar part of the taskbar displays the date and status icons. For example, if you are printing, you see a printer icon in this area.

End

INTRODUCTION

The desktop is your starting place, what you see when you first start your computer and Windows XP. This opening screen provides access to all the programs and files on your computer. This task introduces the main parts of your desktop.

Change the Desktop Background
You can change the appearance of this background. See Part 10, "Personalizing Windows," for more help on changing the appearance of the desktop.

Add Desktop Icons
By default, the Windows XP displays the Recycle Bin. You can also display the My Documents folder and the My Computer icon, as shown here. For help on adding these particular icons to the desktop, see Part 10.

drag

How to Drag:
Point to the starting place or object. Hold down the mouse button (right or left per instructions), move the mouse to the new location, then release the button.

drop

Introductions explain what you will learn in each task, and **Tips and Hints** give you a heads-up for any extra information you may need while working through the task.

See next page

See next page:
If you see this symbol, it means the task you're working on continues on the next page.

End

End Task:
Task is complete.

Selection:
Highlights the area onscreen discussed in the step or task.

Click:
Click the left mouse button once.

Right-click:
Click the right mouse button once.

Click & Type:
Click once where indicated and begin typing to enter your text or data.

Double-click:
Click the left mouse button twice in rapid succession.

Pointer Arrow:
Highlights an item on the screen you need to point to or focus on in the step or task.

Introduction

Access is a database program that enables you to store information such as a client list, products, invoices, inventory, events, and other collections of data. In addition to entering the data in a database table, you have several tools for working with the data. You can create forms for simpler data entry. You can create a query to display a set of records (all customers with over-due balances, for instance). You can create a report. All these elements are Access objects and are stored together in the database.

To help you get started with Access, this book contains parts that explain the basics of using the program, steps on how to create and edit tables, and tasks on modifying the database design, as well as parts on creating and using forms, queries, and reports. Every process is broken down into easy-to-follow steps with illustrations (screen shots) of the process.

As you work through this book, consider key concepts:

- You can work in two views for most objects: Design view and Working view. Think of Design view as viewing the blueprint of a house, whereas Working view is the house itself. In Design view, you can see how the underlying structure creates that object, and you can make changes to the layout. In Working view, you can view and work with your data using the structure you created in Design view. Working view varies depending on the object type. For instance, when working with tables, the view is called Datasheet view. When working with queries, you see the results of the query.

- Each element in a database table is called a *field* and has a field name and data type. One set of fields is a *record*. Although you can make modifications to a database design after you've entered records, you may lose data or encounter a few problems. Therefore, it's a good idea to carefully think about and plan your database structure. Which fields are needed? How do the fields relate? Do I need to break down a field into smaller elements? For instance, it's not a good idea to include one field for a person's name. Instead, include a first name field and a last name field. This setup makes sorting and searching easier.

- When you are entering data, you do not need to save your work. Access saves the work automatically. When you create or modify an object such as a database table, form, or report, you *do* need to save your changes.

- Rather than store all your data in one large database table, you can break down the information into separate tables and then set up relationships between the tables. For instance, rather than have a table that includes products, orders, and customer names, you can include separate tables for each and then link them. (Working with multiple tables is a topic of Part 8.)

Access is a high-powered tool and includes elements that enable you to create a customized database program. This book gets you started on the basics of using Access. To learn about some of the more advanced features, consider a reference book such as *Using Access*.

Learning Access Basics

This section covers the basic tools and options you'll find in Access 2003. Here, you'll learn how to start the program, how to use the toolbars and menus, and more. Learning these basics will help you not only with using the various features included with Access but also with using all Windows-based programs.

Database Window

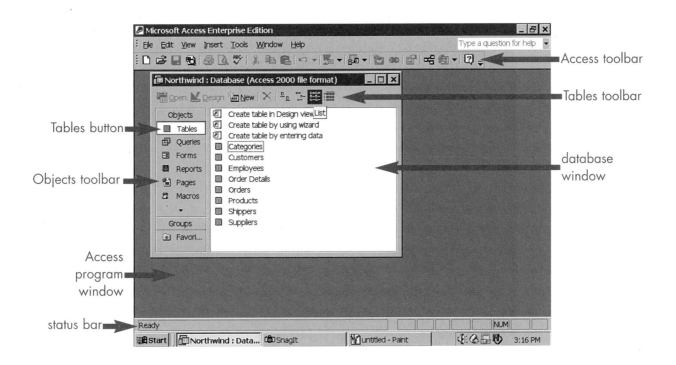

Starting Access

Click

① Move the mouse pointer to the **Start** button on the taskbar. A ToolTip appears that reads **Click here to begin**.

② Click the **Start** button to see the **Start** menu. (Depending on which programs are installed on your computer, your menu may look slightly different from the one shown here.)

TIP

Finding the Taskbar
If you don't see the taskbar right away, it may be hidden. Move your mouse to the bottom of the screen to bring it into view. Alternatively, the taskbar may simply be docked at the top or on the left or right side of the screen.

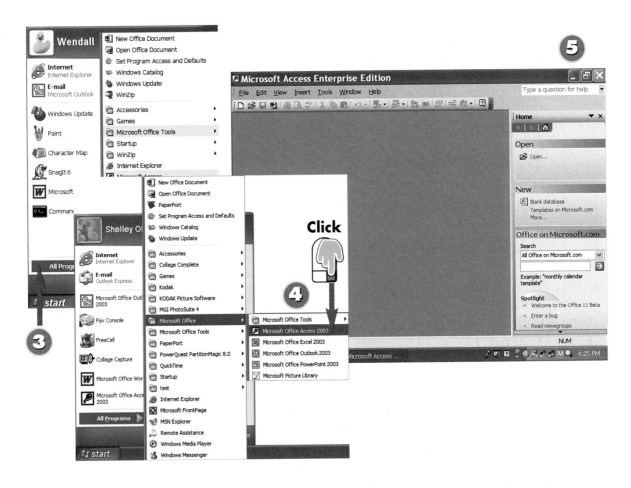

3 Move the mouse pointer to the **All Programs** menu option.

4 Move the mouse pointer across the menu and click Microsoft Office (if necessary) and then **Microsoft Access**.

5 Access opens with a blank background and a Task pane on the right side of the screen.

End

Starting Shortcuts

TIP

If you have added a desktop shortcut for Access, you can double-click this shortcut to start the program. Also, if Access is one of your frequently used programs, you may see it listed on the left pane of the Start menu. You can click it from this list to start it. Finally, you may also see a Quick Launch toolbar displayed in the Windows taskbar. You can use the buttons in this toolbar to launch Office programs as well.

Opening a Sample Database

Start

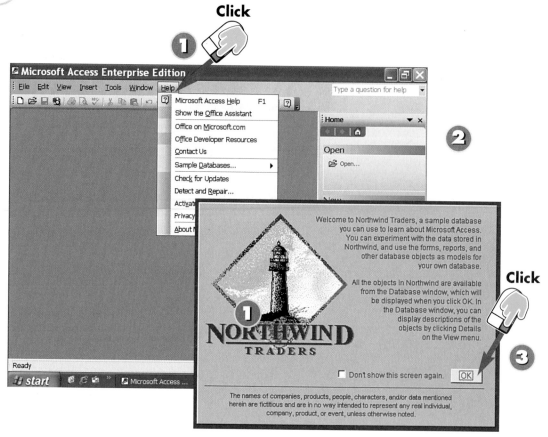

Click

1

2

Click

3

① To open a sample database, begin by clicking on the **Help** menu.

② Move the mouse to the **Sample Databases** entry, and click the **Northwind Sample Database** option.

③ The Northwind database's opening screen appears; click **OK** to close this screen and display the Northwind database.

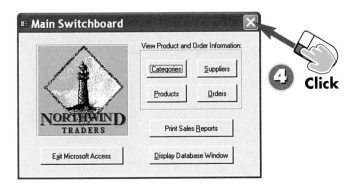

4 The Main Switchboard dialog box opens; click the **Close** button in the upper-right corner of the dialog box to close it.

5 The database window for the Northwind sample database opens. The rest of the tasks in this part show you how to work with an open Access database.

End

Using the Menu Bar

Start

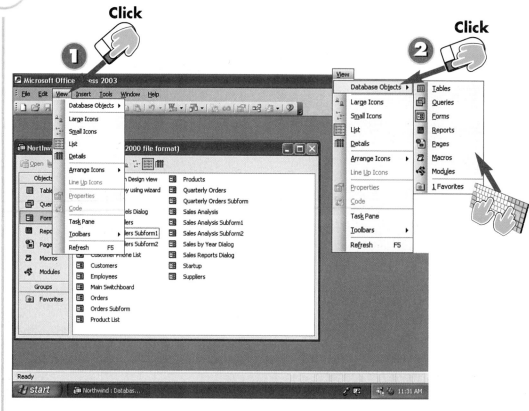

Click

Click

---

1 Click the **View** option in the menu bar. The View menu opens.

2 Click the **Database Objects** entry. A submenu appears, listing additional commands; click any of these commands to select them.

3 Press the **Esc** key on your keyboard or click anywhere outside the open menu. Doing so closes the menu without making a selection.

The menu bar, located at the top of the Access window, displays Access's menus. Simply put, a menu is a list of commands or actions that you can perform.

TIP

Using Personalized Menus
By default, Access displays in its menus only the commands you use most frequently. You'll see an arrow at the bottom of each menu, which you can click to display a complete list of commands. To always display full menus (as shown in this book), open the **Tools** menu and choose **Customize**. Click the **Options** tab, click the **Always show full menus** option to select it, and click **OK**.

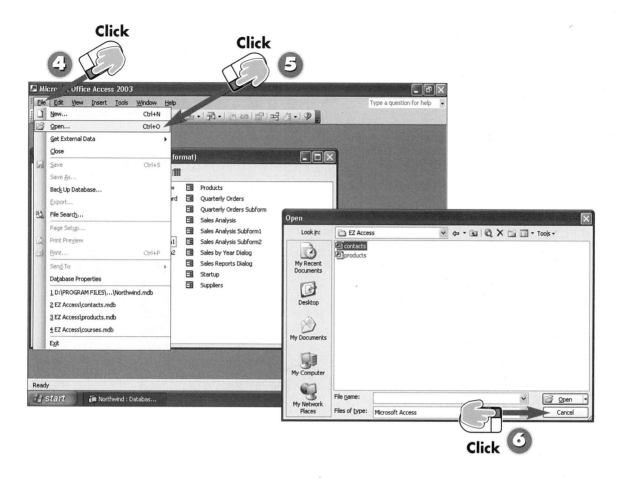

Click ④

Click ⑤

Click ⑥

④ Click the **File** option in the menu bar. The File menu opens.

⑤ Click the **Open** command. Notice that this command is followed by an ellipsis; this indicates that selecting the command will open a dialog box that prompts you for additional information.

⑥ The Open dialog box opens. Here you can select the folder that contains the file you want to open, and then the file. Click **Cancel** to close the dialog box without opening a file.

End

Keyboard Shortcuts
Common actions have special keyboard shortcuts. For instance, to copy a selection, you can press **Ctrl+C**; press **Ctrl+X** to cut a selection; and press **Ctrl+V** to paste a selection.

Using Toolbars

Start

Click

①

Click

②

① Click a toolbar button. For example, to change how objects are displayed in the database window, click the **Large Icons** button to view the table list entries as large icons.

② Click the **Small Icons** button, located next to the Large Icons button, to view the table list entries as small icons.

Click

3

Click

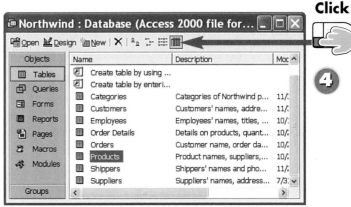

4

3 Click the **List** button, next to the Small Icons button, to view the table entries in a simple list format.

4 Click the **Display** button next to the List button, to view the details of each table in the list, including its description, size, and modification date.

End

Using the Objects Bar

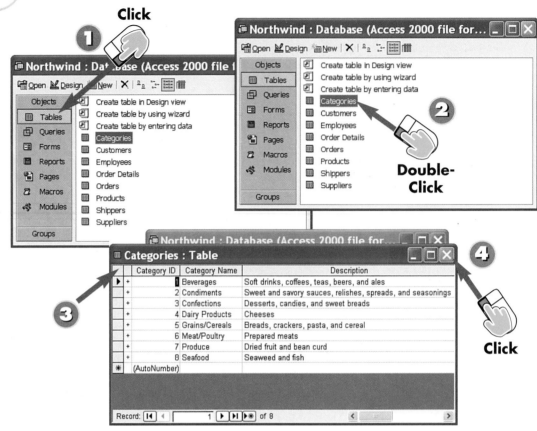

To view table objects in the open database, click the **Tables** button on the Objects bar. A list of tables in the open database appears, as well as commands for creating new tables.

To open any of the listed tables, double-click its name. For instance, double-click the **Categories** entry to open the Categories table.

The Categories table opens. The names at the top of each column identify the data, and each row is a record. (You learn more about tables later in this book.)

Close the Categories table by clicking the **Close** button in the upper-right corner of the table window.

INTRODUCTION

The Objects bar that appears on the left side of the Database window includes buttons for viewing tables, queries, forms, reports, pages, macros, and modules—the same as the entries that appear on the View menu. All the options in the Objects bar represent types of objects that you can create and use in Access. You'll learn how to create most of the types of objects found here in later parts of this book. Any time you want to create, view, or modify an object, you must first select that object type from the View menu or the Objects bar.

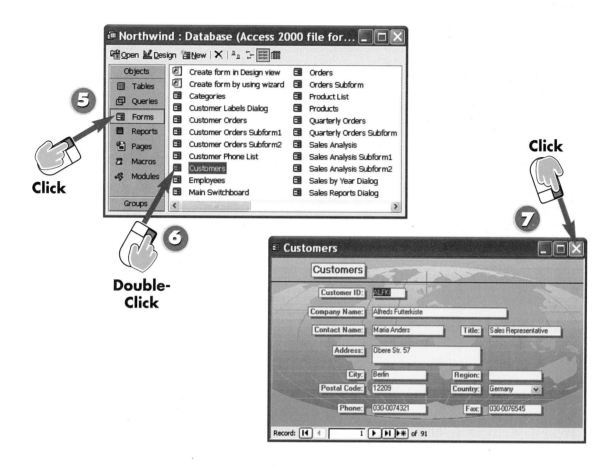

Click

Double-Click

Click

5 Click the **Forms** button on the Objects bar. A list of forms in the open database appears, as well as commands for creating new forms.

6 To open any of the listed forms, double-click its name. For example, double-click the **Customers** form.

7 The Customers form is opened. To close the form, click the **Close** button in the upper-right corner of the form window.

End

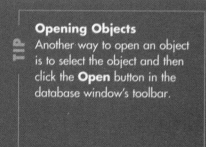

Opening Objects
Another way to open an object is to select the object and then click the **Open** button in the database window's toolbar.

Opening Queries and Reports
You open queries and reports in the same way you do forms and tables: by clicking the **Queries** or **Reports** button in the Objects bar, and then choosing the query or report you need.

Getting Help

Start

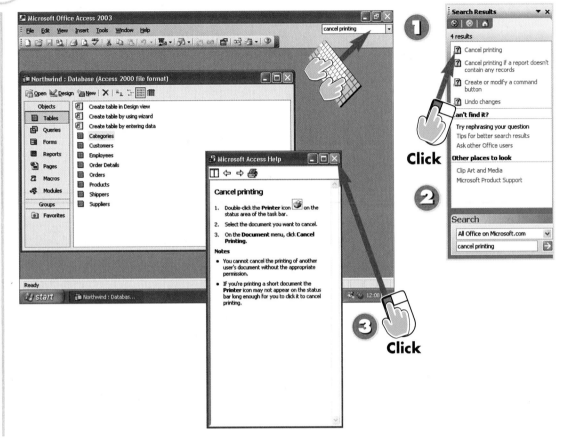

Click

Click

1. In the help box on the menu bar, type **cancel printing** and press **Enter**.

2. A Search Results task pane opens, displaying Help topics that contain the search phrase you entered in step 1. Click the **Cancel printing** entry.

3. A window containing the Help information opens. Read the information in the window, and click the **Close** button in the window's upper-right corner to close it.

INTRODUCTION

Access includes an easy-to-use Help system. One way to access Help is to type a question in the help box found on the right side of the menu bar; another is to use the Help menu. In this task, you'll find out how to use both of these tools to get help canceling a print job.

Search Window Options
TIP Use options in the Search Results task pane to try other matches, get search tips, rephrase the search, or search online. Use Help window options to print the help information, view related links, and go back and forth among viewed topics.

Maximizing the Window
TIP If necessary, click the Help window's **Maximize** button to see more of the help information.

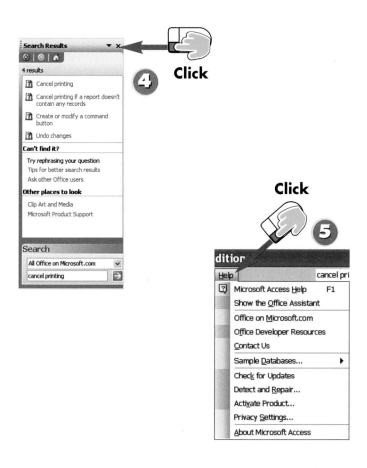

Click

Click

④ To close the Search Results pane, click the **Close** button in its upper-right corner.

⑤ Another way to get help is using the Help menu. Click **Help** on menu bar and choose **Microsoft Access Help** from the menu that appears. (Alternatively, press F1 on your keyboard.)

⑥ The Microsoft Access Help pane opens; type **cancel printing** in the Search box and press **Enter**. You see the same results as you did when you searched using the help box.

End

TIP

Using What's This?
Another way to find help in Microsoft Access is to use the program's What's This? feature. To do so, press the **F1** key on your keyboard; the mouse pointer changes to an arrow with a question mark. Then, click an object about which you want to find information; in most cases, a description of the object appears. Close the description by clicking on another part of the screen or by pressing the **Esc** key.

Closing a Database

Start

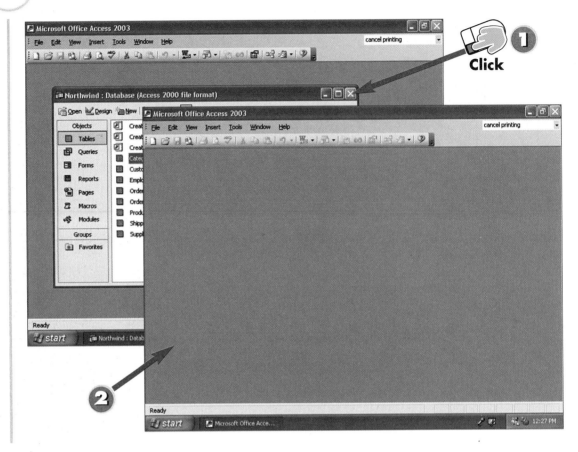

Click

1. To close an open database, click the **Close** button in the upper-right corner of the database window.

2. The database window and database are closed.

End

INTRODUCTION

When you are finished working with a database, you can close it. Doing so frees up memory for other programs you may have open. Keep in mind that you can close a database, but still keep Access open. A database window has its own **Close** button.

NOTE

Saving Your Work
Access is different from other Office applications, in that you will not automatically be asked whether you want to save data entered in a database when you close it; that data will be saved by default. The only time you are prompted to save your work upon closing a database is when structural changes, such as the creation of an object, have been made to that database.

Quitting Access

Start

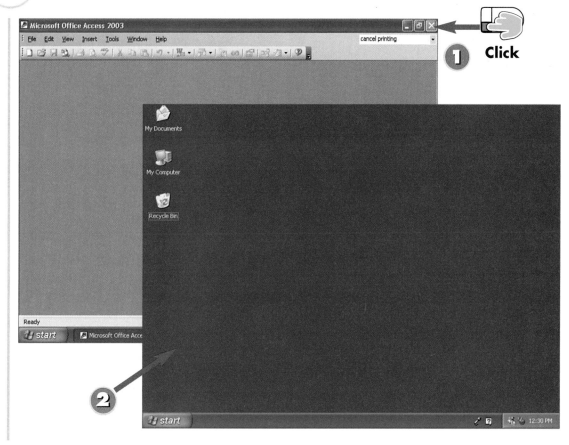

Click

1 To close Access, click the **Close** button in the upper-right corner of the program window.

2 Access is closed.

End

INTRODUCTION

When you're finished using Access, shut it down to conserve system resources. Doing so is a one-click operation.

NOTE

Using a Menu
If you prefer to use menus, you can exit Access by opening the File menu and choosing **Exit**.

Creating Databases and Tables

To use Access, you start by creating a database. Within that database, you can then create tables, forms, reports, and other Access objects that help you organize your data. To help you quickly and easily create a database, Access 2003 includes several database templates, including the Asset Tracking, Event Management, and Time and Billing databases, to name a few. A database template is a predesigned database and contains objects such as tables, reports, and queries for that type of database. If none of the templates suits your needs, you can create a new blank database from scratch.

In addition to providing templates that you can use to create your database, Access 2003 also includes wizards to step you through the creation of commonly used tables. If none of the wizards will work for the type of table you want to create, you can create a blank table from scratch. This part focuses on these key Access tasks—creating a database and creating a database table.

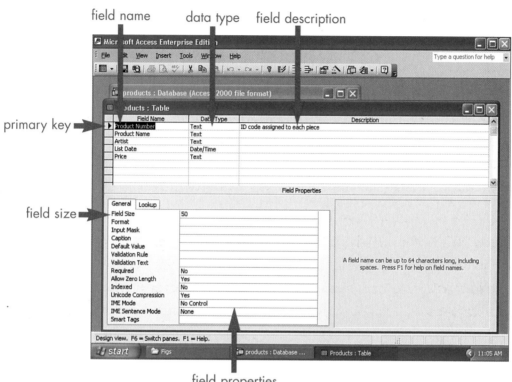

field name   data type   field description

primary key ▶

field size ◀■

field properties

Creating a Database from a Template

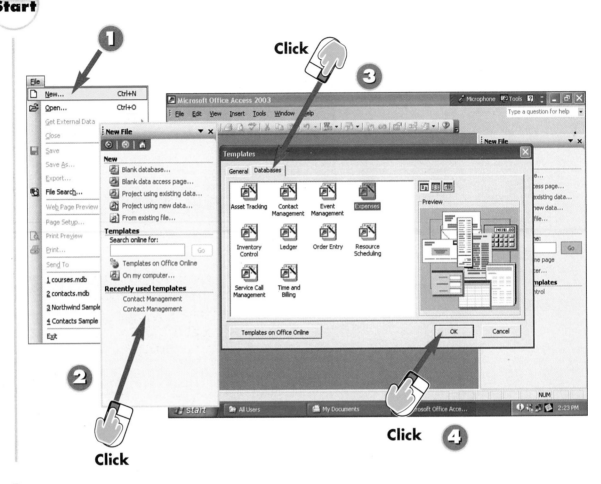

Start

Click ③

Click ②

Click ④

1️⃣ If the New File Task pane is not displayed, open the **File** menu and choose **New**.

2️⃣ In the **Templates** area of the New File Task pane, click the **On my computer** link.

3️⃣ The Templates dialog box opens, displaying the templates installed on your computer. Click the **Databases** tab.

4️⃣ Click the template you want to use and click **OK**.

Access 2003 provides numerous database templates, which you can use to create your database. These database templates are especially handy if you are trying to set up a database quickly. When you elect to create a database from a template, Access launches a wizard that walks you through the process of creating the database. The resulting database includes predesigned tables, forms, queries, and reports. After you have set up the database with a wizard, you can modify any of the database objects as needed; these topics are covered in later parts in this book.

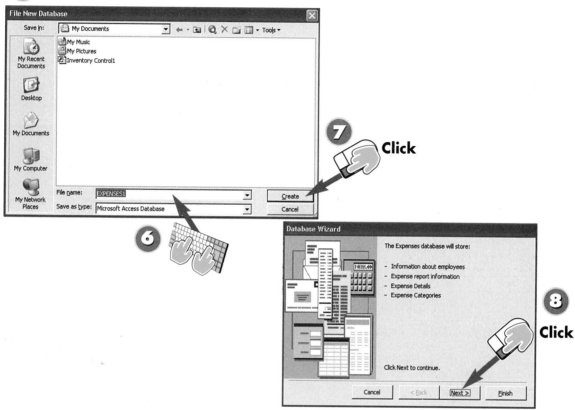

Click

Click

5. The File New Database dialog box opens. Navigate to the folder in which you want to store the new database.

6. In the **File name** field, type a filename for the new database.

7. Click the **Create** button.

8. The Database Wizard starts; after you review what types of data the new database will contain, click the **Next** button.

See next page

TIP

Changing Folders
To change to another folder in the File New Database dialog box, choose a folder from the **Save in** drop-down list, double-click any of the folders listed in the dialog box, click the **Up One Level** button to move up through the folder structure, or click one of the commonly used folders in the **Places** bar.

NOTE

Saving the Database
When you create a new database, you start by assigning a filename to it and selecting the folder in which it will be stored. Within this main database file, you then save the various database objects (tables, forms, etc.).

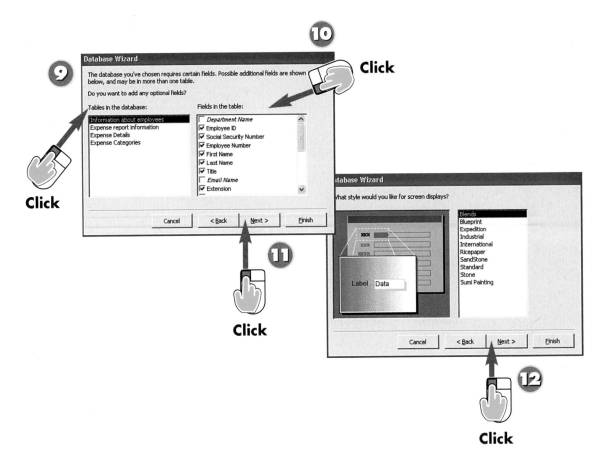

9 A list of the tables included in the new database appears. Click each table in the **Tables in the database** list to view the available fields for that table.

10 If you are certain that your database doesn't require a particular field, click the check box next to the field in the **Fields in the table** list to deselect it.

11 After you have deselected any fields you do not want to include, click **Next**.

12 The wizard presents a list of styles that affect how data in your database is displayed onscreen. Click a style to preview it. When you find one you like, click **Next**.

CAUTION
Deselecting Fields
Although you can choose to deselect fields for the tables in your database, it's usually best to set up databases using their default settings and then modify them as needed later on.

TIP
Change Your Mind?
If you need to make a change to one of your earlier selections, click the **Back** button in the Database Wizard dialog box. You can also click **Cancel** to exit the wizard without creating the database.

TIP
Adding a Picture
To include a picture on your reports (such as a company logo), check the **Yes, I'd like to include a picture** check box (step 14) and then click the **Picture** button. Navigate to the drive and folder that contain the picture file, click the picture to select it, and click **OK**.

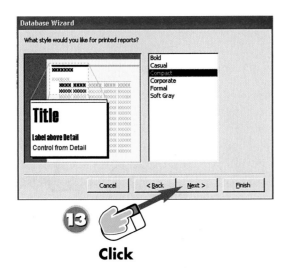

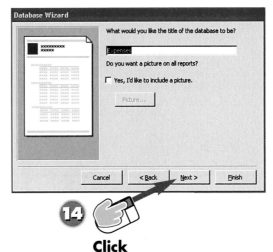

Click **13**

Click **14**

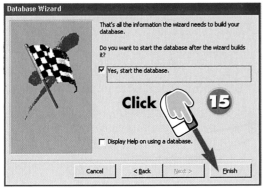

Click **15**

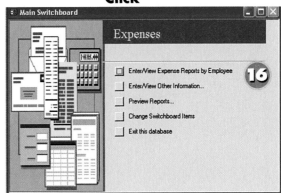

13 The Database Wizard prompts you to select a style for your reports. Click a style to preview it. When you find one you like, click **Next**.

14 Access suggests a title for the new database. If you want, type over the suggested title with one of your own. When you're satisfied with the title, click **Next**.

15 Leave the **Yes, start the database** check box checked, and click **Finish** to create the database.

16 The Main Switchboard window for the new database appears. You can select any of the links in the window, such as **Enter/View Attendees**, to continue building your database.

End

TIP
Using the Switchboard
When you use a template Access displays a Main Switchboard that enables you to click links to perform common database tasks. Click the window's **Close** button to close it and use the database window instead.

TIP
Entering Company Information
For some database templates, you may be prompted to enter company information after you click the wizard's **Finish** button. If prompted, enter the appropriate information.

TIP
Creating Reports
You can also use Access to create reports (the topic of Part 7). As part of using the wizard, you select a particular style for all your reports. You can always modify the style, as covered in Part 7.

Creating a New Blank Database

Start

1

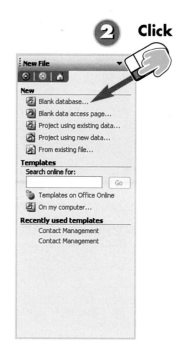

2 **Click**

1 If the New File Task pane is not displayed, open the **File** menu and choose **New**.

2 In the **New** area of the New File Task pane, click the **Blank database** link.

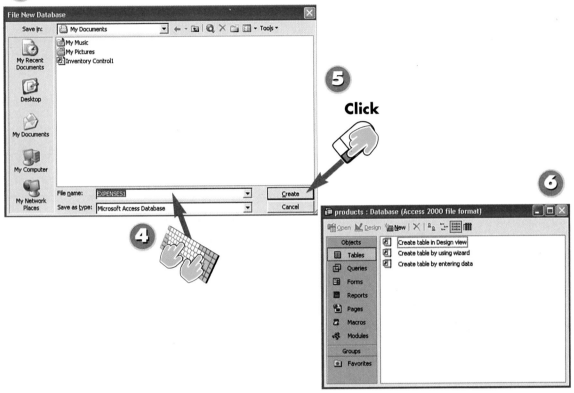

The File New Database dialog box opens. Navigate to the folder in which you want to store the new database.

Type a descriptive name for the new database in the **File name** field.

Click the **Create** button.

Access creates a new database and displays the database window. You create the objects for this new database, such as tables (covered later in this part) and forms, by hand.

End

Opening an Existing Database

Start

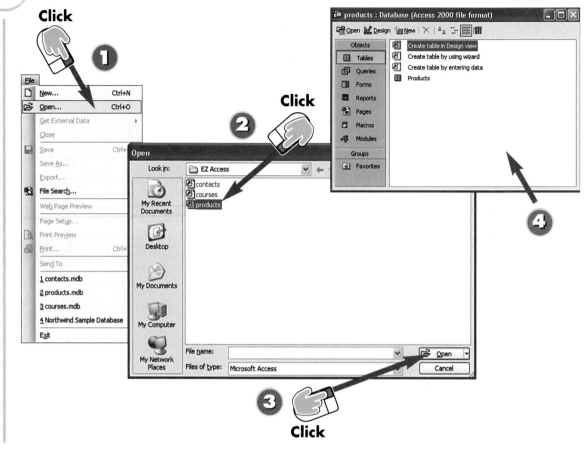

Click ①

Click ②

Click ③

④

---

① Open the **File** menu and choose **Open**.

② The Open dialog box opens. Navigate to the drive and folder that contain the database file you want to work with; click the file to select it.

③ Click the **Open** button.

④ The database window for the selected database opens.

End

INTRODUCTION

After you've created a database, you might later decide you want to modify it—perhaps to create a new table, enter data in a table, modify a table structure, or create other database objects. Before you do, however, you'll need to open the database you want to work with.

TIP

Changing Drives and Folders
Use the **Look in** drop-down list, the Places bar, or the Up One Level button to change to another drive or folder.

Creating a Table Using a Wizard

 Start

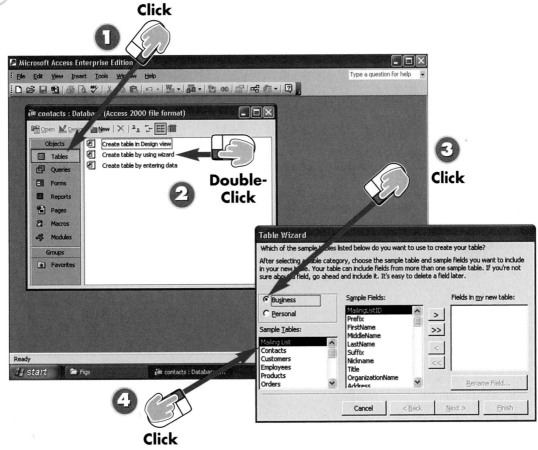

Click ①

Double-Click ②

Click ③

Click ④

① After you've created or opened the database for which you want to create a table, click the **Tables** option in the Objects bar in the database window.

② Double-click the **Create table by using wizard** option.

③ The first screen of the Table Wizard opens. Click either the **Business** or the **Personal** option button to specify how your database will be used.

④ The **Sample Tables** list contains available sample tables for the table type you selected in step 3. Click the type of table you want to create.

 See next page

INTRODUCTION

The main structure of a database is a *table*. A database can contain any number of tables. Each table in a database consists of *fields* (an individual piece of data) and *records* (a set of fields). After you create a database, you then start building the tables it will contain. To help you get started, you can use one of Access's wizards, selecting from many common table types including mailing lists, contacts, products, orders, events, projects, and others.

TIP

Opening the Database
If the database for which you want to create a table is not currently open, you can open it. See the preceding task to learn how.

Creating a Table Using a Wizard (Continued)

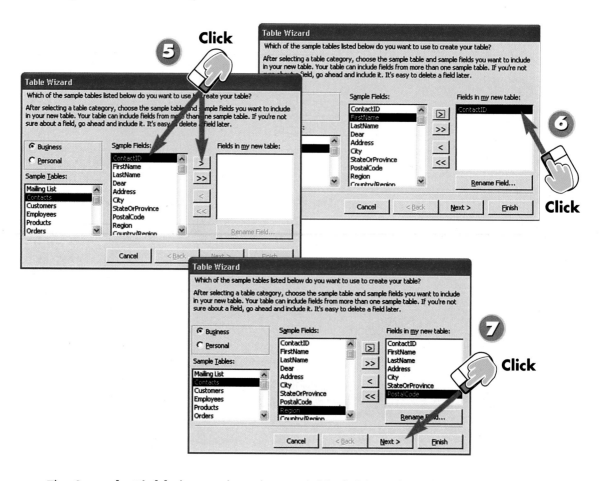

Click

Click

Click

The **Sample Fields** list catalogs the available fields in the selected sample table. Click the first field you want to include in your table, and click the **Add** (right arrow) button.

The field is added to the **Fields in my new table** list. Repeat step 5 to continue adding fields to your table until it contains all the fields you want to include.

Click the **Next** button.

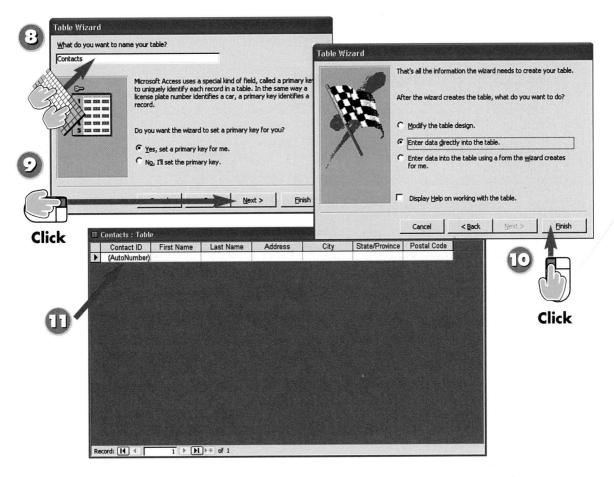

Click

Click

(8) Type a name for the table.

(9) Access asks whether you want the wizard to set the primary key for you; the default setting is **Yes, set a primary key for me**. Keep this option selected and click **Next**.

(10) The wizard prompts you to select the next action; the default setting is **Enter data directly into the table**. Keep this option selected and click **Finish**.

(11) The new database table is created and displayed onscreen, ready for you to begin entering records. (See Part 3 for help entering data.)

End

Setting the Primary Key

As you saw in step 9, you can let Access set the table's primary key for you. The *primary key* is a field that uniquely identifies each record in the database and is used for sorting and indexing. If necessary, you can change the primary key or create a new one. See the task "Setting the Primary Key" later in this part for more information.

Customizing Fields

If the table does not include all the fields you need, you can add new fields later. You can also delete and rename fields as needed. You'll learn how later in this part.

Creating a Database Table from Scratch

Start

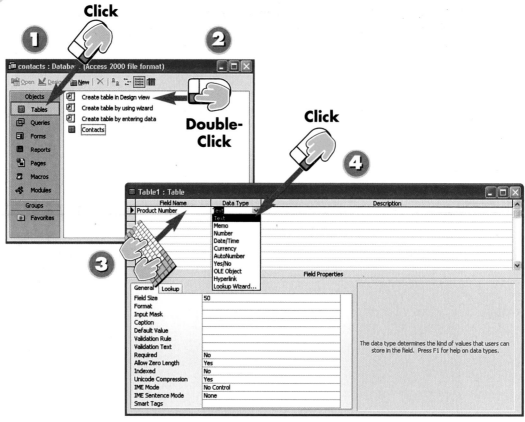

1. After you've created or opened the database for which you want to create a table, click the **Tables** option in the Objects bar in the database window.

2. Double-click the **Create table in Design view** option.

3. A blank table opens in Design view, containing Field Name, Data Type, and Description columns. In the **Field Name** column, type a name for the first field and then press **Tab**.

4. To change the data type from the default, Text, click the **down arrow** in the **Data Type** field and choose a new data type from the list that appears. Then press **Tab**.

There may be times when you want to create a table from scratch instead of using Access's Table Wizard. In this case, you create a blank table and then create each of the fields by hand—typing a field name, selecting a data type, and, optionally, entering a field description. You can include as many fields as needed in your table.

TIP

Understanding Field Names
You must use a unique name for each field in your table, and it's a good idea to use descriptive names that remind you of the contents of that field. A field name can include as many as 64 characters.

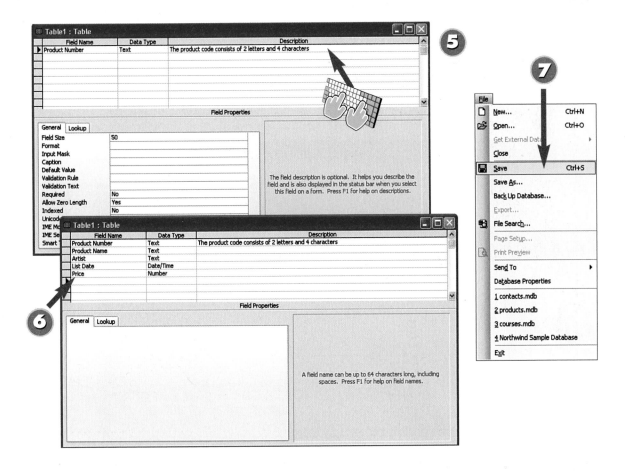

5 Optionally, type a field description in the **Description** column. This text appears in the Table window's status bar when you are entering data and this field is selected.

6 Repeat steps 3–5 as needed to continue adding fields.

7 To save the table, open the **File** menu and choose **Save**.

See next page

Understanding Data Types

TIP

For more information about the available data types, see "Setting a Field's Data Type" later in this part. In addition, Part 4 covers creating special data types.

Creating a Database Table from Scratch (Continued)

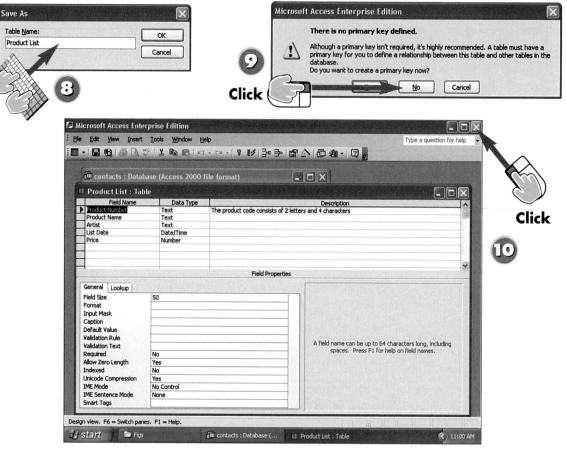

8 The Save As dialog box opens. Type a name for the table and click **OK**.

9 Access prompts you to set a primary key. Click **No** to set the primary key later.

10 The table is saved, and the name you typed in step 9 appears in the table window's title bar. To close the table window and return to the database window, click the **Close** button.

End

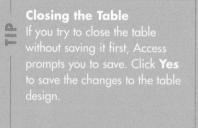

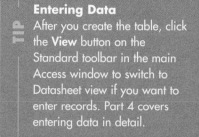

TIP
Saving Tables
The table is saved as part of the database file.

TIP
Closing the Table
If you try to close the table without saving it first, Access prompts you to save. Click **Yes** to save the changes to the table design.

TIP
Entering Data
After you create the table, click the **View** button on the Standard toolbar in the main Access window to switch to Datasheet view if you want to enter records. Part 4 covers entering data in detail.

Displaying a Table in Design View

Start

Click ① **Click** ③

④

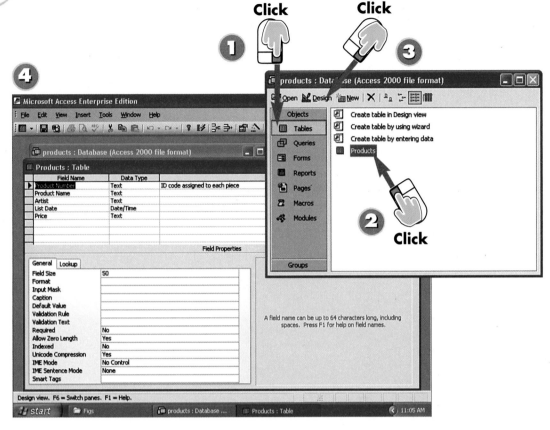

Click ②

After you've created or opened the database that contains the table you want to modify, click the **Tables** option in the Objects bar in the database window.

② Click the table you want to open to select it.

③ Click the **Design** button in the database window's toolbar.

④ The table is open in Design view, enabling you to make changes to the database structure.

End

If you create a table using a wizard, you may find that you need to customize the fields it contains—adding new fields, removing fields, or modifying the properties of a particular field (such as its size). Even if you create a table from scratch, you may later find that you need to modify it in some way. Before you can modify a table, you must open that table in Design view. (Design view contrasts with Datasheet view, which you use to enter data.)

Entering Data

TIP

To open a table in Datasheet view, double-click the table name in the database window or click the table to select it and then click the **Open** button in the database window's toolbar. See Part 3 for more information about entering data.

Adding a New Field

Start

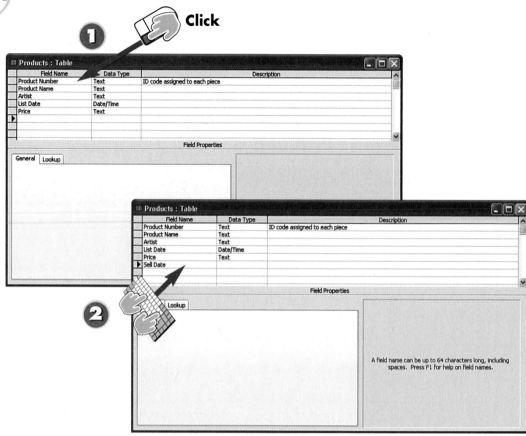

Click

1 After you've opened the table you want to modify in Design view, click in the **Field Name** column of the first empty row.

2 Type a name for the field and press **Tab**.

It's best to plan out the structure of your table before you build it, mapping out the various pieces of data you need to store and then figuring out what fields you need to store them. If needed, though, you can add a new field at any time. For example, you might need to add a field if you used a wizard to create your table and the default fields did not include all the entries you needed. Or, you might need to add a new field if you created a table from scratch and accidentally left out something.

Inserting Rows

TIP

If you want to add a new field to the middle of your table, rather than to the end, you can do so. Click in the row below the spot where you want the new row to be, open the **Insert** menu, and choose **Rows**. The new row is inserted below the selected row.

Click

Click

3

5

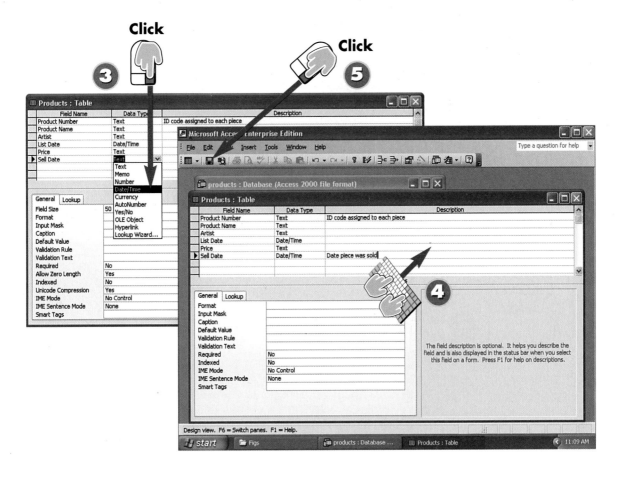

3 To change the data type from the default, Text, click the **down arrow** in the **Data Type** field and choose a new data type from the list that appears. Then press **Tab**.

4 Optionally, type a field description in the **Description** column. This text appears in the Table window's status bar when you are entering data and this field is selected.

5 Click the **Save** button on the Standard toolbar in the main Access window to save your changes to the database table.

End

TIP
Understanding Field Names
You must use a unique name for each field in your table, and it's a good idea to use descriptive names that remind you of the contents of that field. A field name can include as many as 64 characters.

TIP
Understanding Data Types
For more information about the available data types, see "Setting a Field's Data Type" later in this part. In addition, Part 4 covers creating special data types.

Changing a Field Name

Start

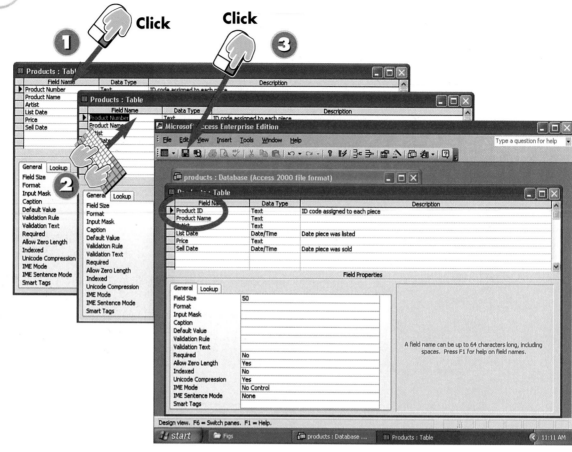

Click ① **Click** ③

1. After you've opened the table you want to modify in Design view, click in the **Field Name** column for the field you want to change.

2. Select the field's current name, and then type over the selection with the new field name.

3. The field's name is changed. Click the **Save** button on the Standard toolbar in the main Access window to save the changes to the table.

End

Each field has a unique name that identifies it. Because these names are used in other Access objects, such as forms and reports, it's wise to use descriptive, yet succinct, names when possible. If you do not like the name you assigned a field, or if a default name assigned by the Table Wizard doesn't suit your needs, you can easily change a field's name.

TIP

Renaming a Field in Datasheet View
You can also rename a field in Datasheet view. To do so, right-click the field's column and select **Rename Column** from the list that appears. Type a new name and then click outside the field name.

Setting a Field's Data Type

Start

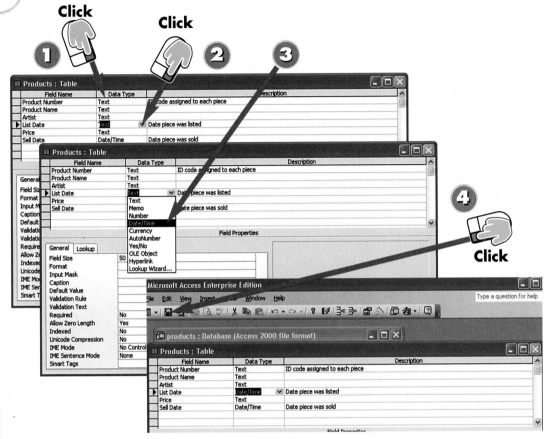

Click

Click

Click

① After you've opened the table you want to modify in Design view, click in the **Data Type** column for the field you want to change.

② To change the data type from the default, Text, click the **down arrow** in the **Data Type** field.

③ Choose a new data type from the list that appears.

④ The field type is changed. Click the **Save** button on the Standard toolbar in the main Access window to save the changes to the table.

End

INTRODUCTION

Chances are, you plan to store many different types of information in your database tables—names, dates, product IDs, financial information, and so on. That's where data types come in; they enable you to specify what type of data a particular field contains. For example, you use the Text data type for fields that contain text (such as names) ; likewise, you use the Number data type for fields that contain numbers (such as product IDs, telephone numbers, and so on) . For dates, you use the Date/Time data type, and for monetary values, you use the Currency data type. Other data types include Memo, AutoNumber, Yes/No, OLE Object, and Hyperlink; you'll learn about some of these in Part 4.

CAUTION

If you have already entered data in the table, changing the field type may result in the loss of your entries. If so, Access will duly notify you, enabling you to choose to make or cancel the change.

Setting the Field Size for a Text Field

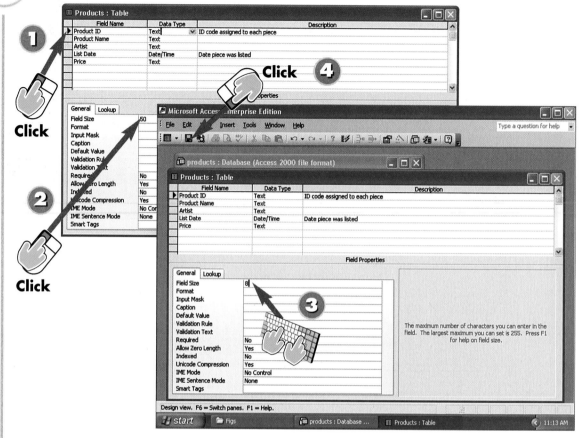

Start

Click ①

Click ②

Click ④

Click ③

---

① After you've opened the table you want to modify in Design view, click the text field whose size you want to change to select it.

② The lower half of the table window shows the properties of the selected field, the first of which for text fields is Field Size. Click the **Field Size** text box.

③ Type the number of characters you want the text field to allow.

④ Click the **Save** button on the Standard toolbar in the main Access window to save your changes to the database table.

End

Text fields (that is, fields that use a Text data type) have a default length of 50 characters, which is usually long enough. To conserve space or to limit the number of characters, however, you may want to change the field size. For example, for a field that contains state abbreviations, you may want to set the field size to 2 so that users can enter only two characters. For longer entries (such as a street address), you may want to increase the field size.

Data Types and Field Sizes

You can change the field size of text and number fields only. Other field types have a default size, which you cannot change.

Setting the Field Size for a Number Field

Start

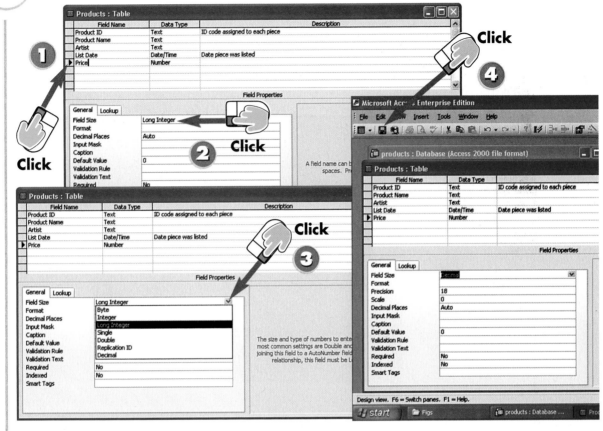

1. After you've opened the table you want to modify in Design view, click the number field whose size you want to change to select it.

2. The lower half of the table window shows the properties of the selected field, the first of which for number fields is the Field Size. Click the **Field Size** text box.

3. Click the **down arrow** that appears in the Field Size text box and select a field size from the list that appears.

4. Click the **Save** button on the Standard toolbar in the main Access window to save your changes to the table.

End

INTRODUCTION

As with text fields, you can also change the size of number fields. Unlike text fields, however, the size of a number field is not tied to the number of characters that field can contain. Instead, Access uses a special name for each available field size. The most common is Long Integer, which is the longest size for a number. (You can store numbers between –2,147,483,648 and 2,147,483,647.)

TIP

Understanding Number Field Sizes
The most common field sizes for numbers are Double and Long Integer. You can, however, use other sizes for special purposes. Consult the online help for detailed instructions on the other sizes and their uses.

Adding a Field Description

Start

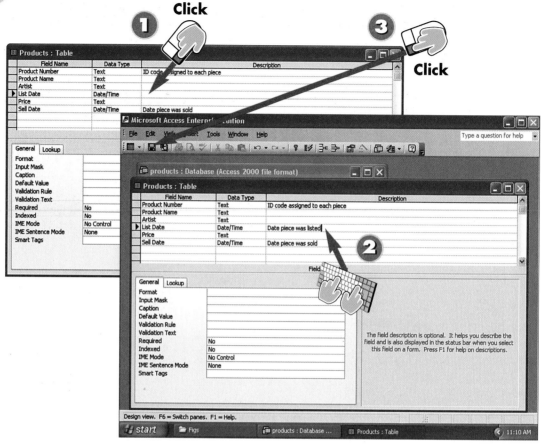

Click 1

Click 3

Click 2

1. After you've opened the table you want to modify in Design view, click in the **Description** column for the field whose Description text you want to add (or change).

2. Type (or edit) the field description.

3. Click the **Save** button on the Standard toolbar in the main Access window to save your changes to the table.

End

Although your table's field names may be quite descriptive, it's good practice to add some additional information about each field for people performing data-entry tasks. A *field description* is useful for this purpose. Using the Description column in the table window, you can type informational phrases or reminders for each field's contents. A field's description appears in the table window's status bar when you are entering data and that field is selected.

Deleting a Field

Start

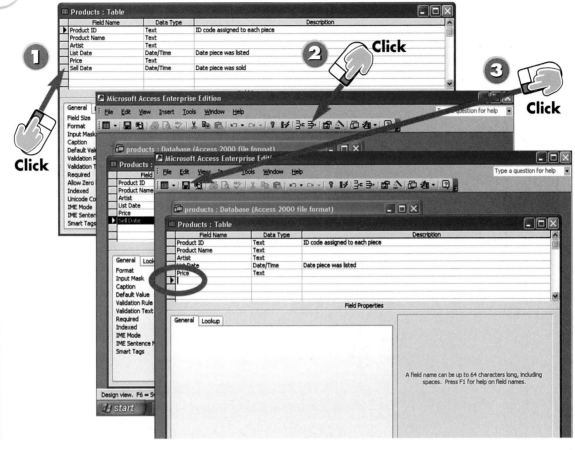

Click

Click

Click

1 After you've opened the table you want to modify in Design view, click the field selector (the leftmost column of the table) for the field you want to delete. A right-facing arrow appears.

2 The field is selected. Click the **Delete Rows** button on the Standard toolbar in the main Access window.

3 The field is deleted. Click the **Save** button on the Standard toolbar in the main Access window to save the changes to your table.

End

INTRODUCTION

If your database includes fields that you do not need, you can delete them. Keep in mind, though, that if you have already entered data into the table, you will lose all the entries in the field you deleted.

Setting the Primary Key

Start

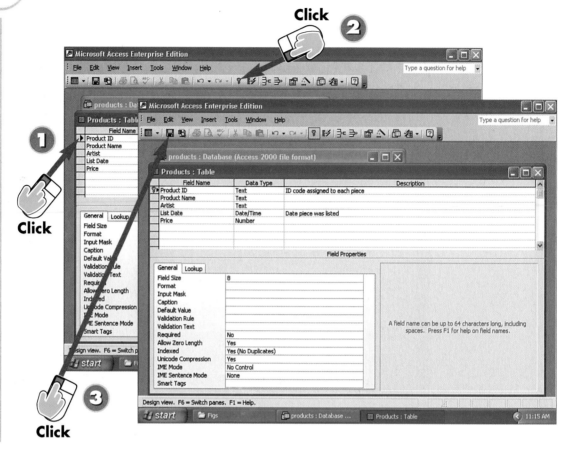

Click

Click

Click

1. After you've opened the table for which you want to set a primary key in Design view, click the field that you want to use as the primary key to select it.

2. Click the **Primary Key** button on the Standard toolbar in the main Access window.

3. Access adds a key icon to the field to indicate that it is the primary key. Click the **Save** button on the Standard toolbar in the main Access window to save your changes to the table.

End

INTRODUCTION

To help ensure that each record in your table is unique, Access encourages you to create a unique ID field and to use this field as the table's *primary key*. The primary key helps with sorting, indexing, and other database functions. In your database, you should set up an ID-type field and then set this field as the primary key. This ID field might contain unique product numbers, Social Security numbers, or even an arbitrary AutoNumber field.

TIP

AutoNumber
If you let Access create the primary key for you, it creates an AutoNumber field that is incremented for every new record you create.

Saving the Data Table

Start

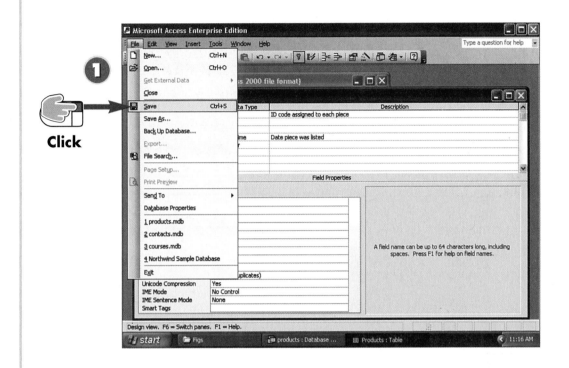

1

Click

---

1 After you make changes to a table's structure, open the **File** menu and choose **Save**. The database table is saved.

End

Entering Data

You create a database and database tables so that you can store your information in a usable format. You might store information about contacts, products, inventory, events, members, invoices, orders, customers, or any other collection of related data. You can set up multiple tables in your database.

In Access, a table is divided into fields, and each field contains one piece of information such as a last name or a price. One completed set of fields is a record. For instance, in a contact database, the name, address, phone, and other entries for one contact is one record.

This part covers how to enter data into a database table, creating the records for your database table. You also learn how to work with the records, edit data, sort records, print data, and so on.

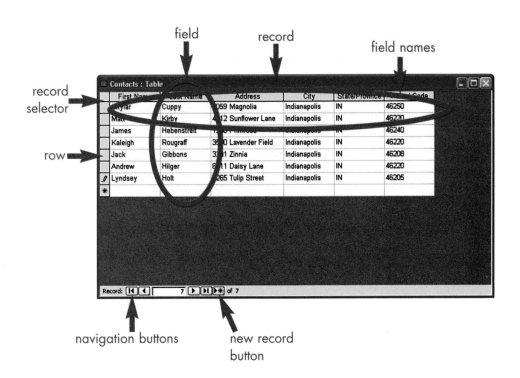

field

record

field names

record selector

row

navigation buttons

new record button

Opening and Closing a Table in Datasheet View

Start

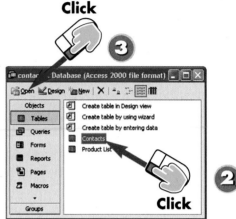

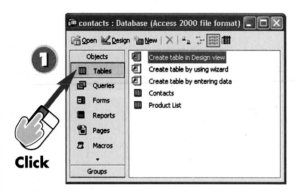

Click

Click

Click

1 After you've opened the database that contains the table you want to open, click the **Tables** option in the Objects bar to display the available tables in that database.

2 Click the table you want to open.

3 Click the **Open** button in the database window's toolbar.

To enter data in a table, you start by opening the table in Datasheet view. Looking at a table in Datasheet view is similar to looking at an Excel worksheet; you see a grid of columns and rows. Each column stores a field, and the column heading is the field name. Each row is a record. From within Datasheet view, you can enter data.

Shortcut

As a shortcut, you can double-click the table in the database window instead of clicking it and then clicking the **Open** button.

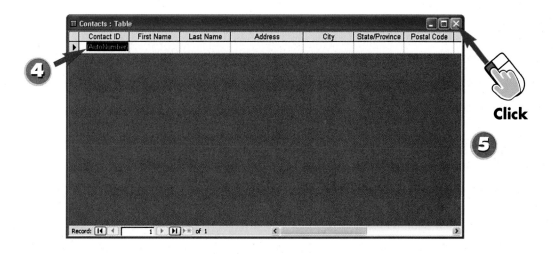

Click

The table opens in Datasheet view. If you have entered records in the table, they are visible; if not, the table is blank.

To close the table window, click its **Close** button.

End

Changing Views
When the table is open, you can click the **Views** button on the Standard toolbar in the main Access window to switch from Datasheet view to Design view and vice versa. You use Design view to alter the structure of the database, discussed in Parts 2 and 4.

Entering Data in a Table

Start

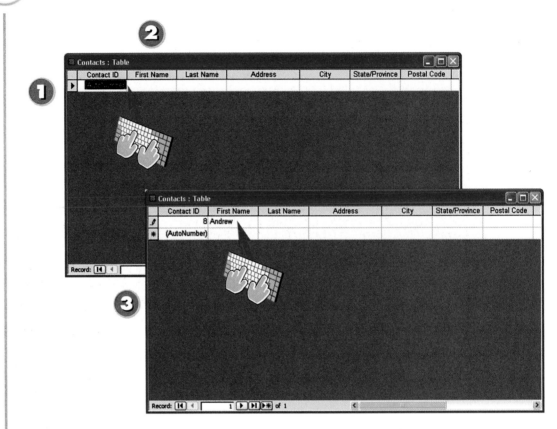

1 Open the table in which you want to enter data. Notice that the first field is selected.

2 If the selected field is an AutoNumber field (shown here), press **Tab** to move to the next field. If not, type an entry in the selected field before pressing the **Tab** key on your keyboard.

3 The insertion point moves to the next field (here, the First Name field). Type an entry (in this case, **Andrew**) and press the **Tab** key.

A database is only as powerful as the data its tables contain. One way to enter data into your database's tables is to use Datasheet view (covered here). This method is much like entering data into an Excel spreadsheet. Another way to enter data into a table is to use a form; you'll learn about creating and using forms in Part 5.

AutoNumber Fields
Some tables may include an AutoNumber field. This type of field contains an incremental number that is automatically entered.

Default Entries
If you set up any default entries for the table (you'll learn how in Part 4), those fields in the table will already be complete. Of course, you can always override the entry by typing a new one.

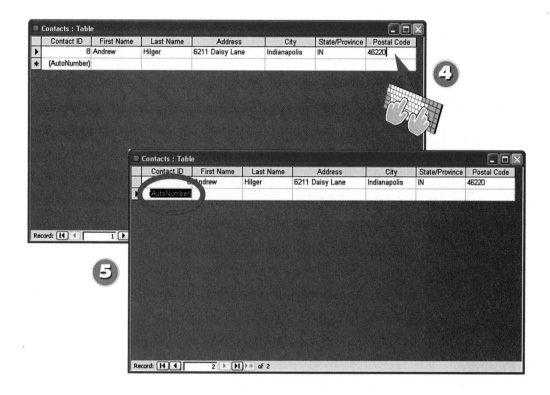

4 The next field is selected. Continue typing entries and pressing the **Tab** key until you complete all the fields in the row, or *record*.

5 When you press **Tab** after completing the last field in the row, Access saves the record and creates a new, blank row, ready for your entries.

End

Saving Your Entries
When entering data, you don't need to use the Save command to save your work. Each time you move the insertion point out of the current record or field, Access automatically saves your work.

"Freezing" Field Names
To help you with data entry, you can "freeze" these column headings so that they are visible at all times, regardless of where you scroll in your table. For more information, see the task "Freezing and Unfreezing Columns" later in this part.

Displaying Records

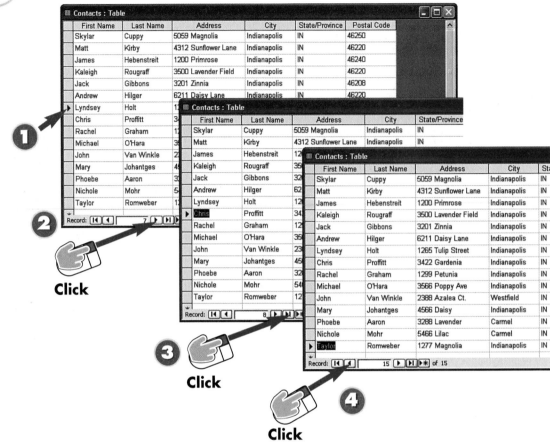

Click

Click

Click

1 Open the table whose records you want to view. An arrow points to the current record, and the navigation bar lists the record's number and the total number of records in the table.

2 To move to the next record in the table, click the **Next Record** button in the navigation bar.

3 The next record in the table is selected. To move to the last record in the table, click the **Last Record** button.

4 The last record in the table (in this case, record 15), is selected. To move to the previous record (that is, record 14), click the **Previous Record** button.

At first, a database table may include just a few records. As you continue to add records, however, that number will grow. To help you view all the records in a table, the table window includes a row of scroll buttons that allow you to scroll up and down in the window in case the record you need is not currently displayed onscreen. Alternatively, you can use the navigation buttons found at the bottom of the table window to move from record to record, as outlined here.

Click

5 The second-to-last record (record 14) is selected. Click the **First Record** button to select the first record in the table.

6 The first record is selected.

End

Adding a New Record
The navigation bar also includes a button for creating a new record. You can click this button or the button in the Standard toolbar in the main Access window to create a new record. See the next task for more information.

Creating a New Record

Start

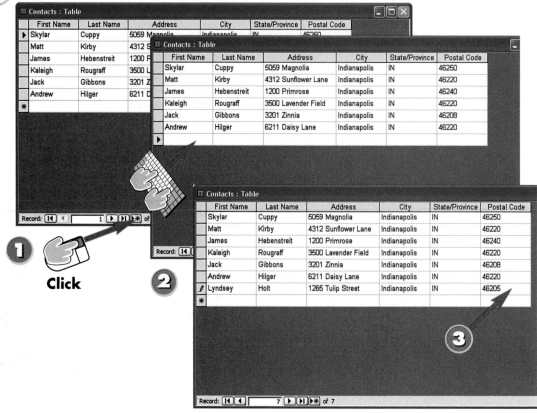

①
Click

②

③

End

① After you've opened the table to which you want to add a new record, click the **New Record** button in the table window's navigation bar.

② Access moves to the first available row in the table and selects the first field. Type the entry for the field, and press **Tab**.

③ Continue typing entries and pressing Tab until you complete the record.

When creating a new table, Access automatically places your insertion point in the first field of a new record. When you press **Tab** after completing the last field in that row, Access saves the record in that row and creates a new, blank record, ready for your entries. That means that the first time you enter data into your table, you don't have to make a special effort to create new records. If, however, you add records to your table at a later date, you'll need to know how to create manually a new row in which to place records.

Scrolling to the Last Row
If you prefer, you can scroll to the end of the table or click the **Last Record** button in the table window's navigation bar to quickly move to the end of the table, which contains a blank row by default. Then, press **Tab** to begin creating a new record.

Selecting an Entry

Start

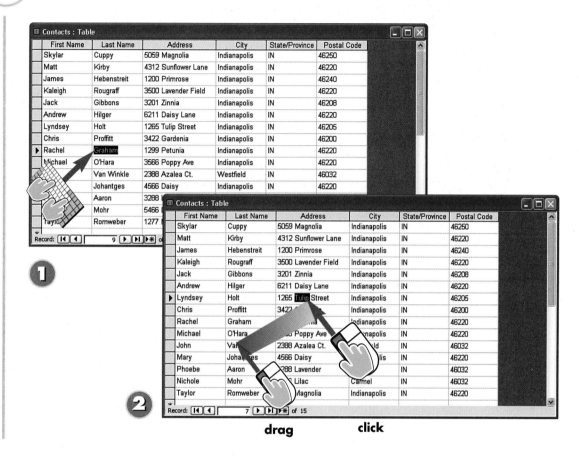

drag   click

1 To select an entire entry, press **Tab** to move to the field containing that entry.

2 To select just part of an entry, click in the field, position the insertion point at the start of the entry you want to select, and click and drag across the desired entry. Just that part is selected.

End

When you want to select the entire entry in a field—for example, to edit or delete that entry—you can press the **Tab** key on your keyboard one or more times to move to the field you want to select. When you reach the field, the entire entry will be selected. If you select an entry and type, any text you type replaces the selected entry. In some cases, however, you may want to select just part of an entry—for example, if you need to change or delete only part of the entry. To select part of an entry, you click in the field and drag to select the entry, similar to how you selects text in a word-processing document.

Using the Keyboard
You can also use the keyboard to select an entry. To do so, move the insertion point to the start of the text you want to select. Press and hold down the **Shift** key, and then use the arrow keys on your keyboard to highlight the text.

Selecting Records and Columns

Start

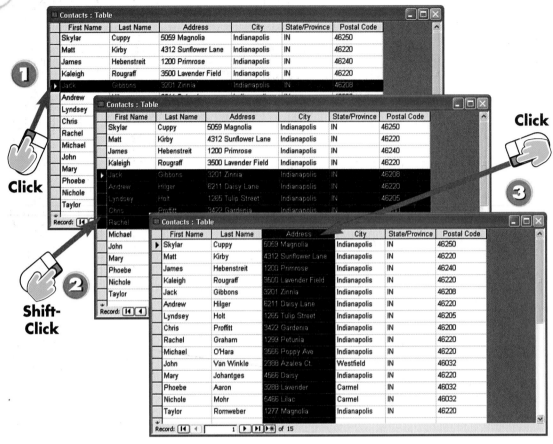

Click

Click

Shift-
Click

1 To select a single record, click the record selector column (the leftmost column in the table). The record is highlighted.

2 To select a block of records, click the record selector column next to the first record in the block, press and hold down the **Shift** key, and click the last record's selector column.

3 To select a column, click the column heading.

End

When you want to work with an entire record—for instance, to edit or delete the record—you must first select the record. You can select a single record or several records at once. You can also select a column to move or delete that field in all the records in that table.

Deselecting Records
To deselect a record, click anywhere in the body of the table.

Selecting All Records
To select all records in a table, open the **Edit** menu and choose **Select All Records**. Alternatively, press **Ctrl+A**.

Freezing and Unfreezing Columns

Start

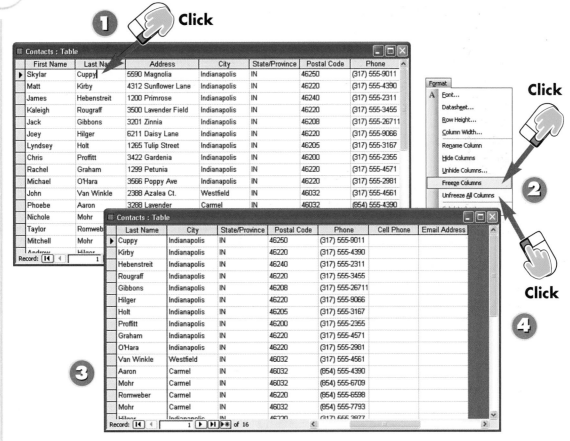

Click

Click

Click

1. Click anywhere in the column you want to freeze.

2. Open the **Format** menu and choose **Freeze Columns**.

3. The column is frozen onscreen. As you scroll to other fields, this frozen column remains in place.

4. To unfreeze the column, open the **Format** menu and choose **Unfreeze All Columns**.

End

Suppose that you're working with a table that contains so many columns that you cannot view all of them onscreen at once. In such cases, entering data can be difficult, because it's easy to lose track of which record you're working with—for example, if you are entering product information but the column containing the product name or ID is not displayed. In that case, you can freeze the product name or ID column so that it remains onscreen at all times. You can also unfreeze them to turn off this feature.

Column Moved?
If the column you selected to freeze is not the first column in the table, Access moves it so that it is the first column. You can move it back to its original location. See the task "Rearranging Columns" later in this part.

Hiding and Unhiding Columns

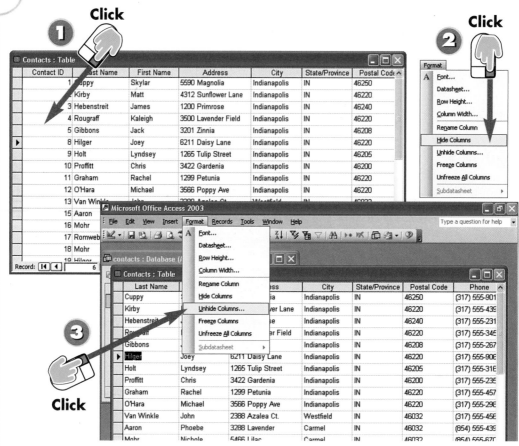

1 Click in the column you want to hide.

2 Open the **Format** menu and choose **Hide Columns**.

3 The column is hidden from view. To redisplay the hidden column, open the **Format** menu and choose **Unhide Columns**.

Another way to focus on certain fields in your table is to hide columns. For example, you can hide columns that already have entries or that are not pertinent to your work at that time. You may also want to hide columns so that you can print just the entries you want. When you are ready to redisplay any columns you have hidden, you can unhide them.

Hiding Several Columns
You can hide several columns at once by first selecting them and then opening the **Format** menu and choosing **Hide Columns**. To select multiple columns, click on the column heading of the first column you want to select and then drag your mouse pointer across all the columns.

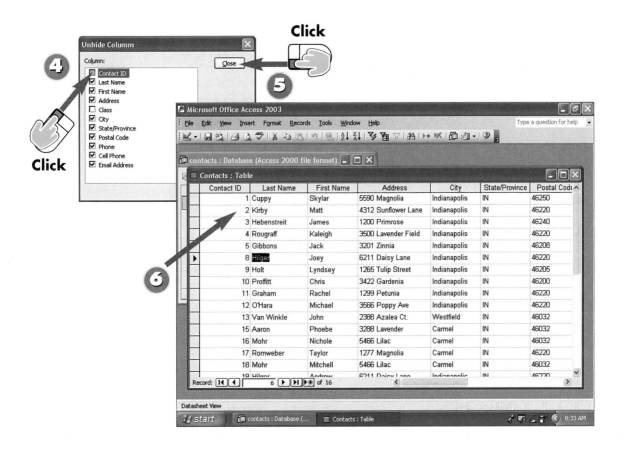

Click

Click

Click

The Unhide Columns dialog box opens, listing the columns in your table. Each column is accompanied by a check box; unchecked columns are hidden. Mark the column's check box to display it.

Click **Close**.

The hidden column (or columns) is redisplayed.

End

Resizing Columns

Start

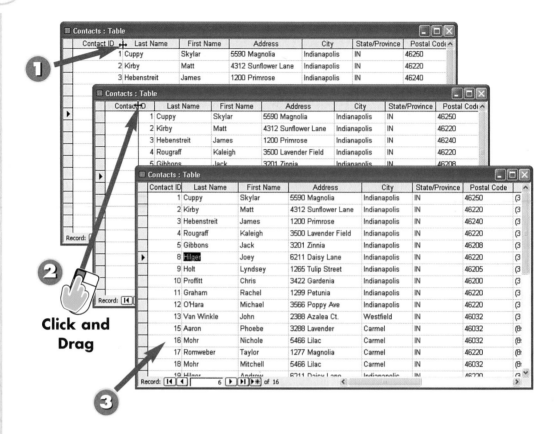

Click and Drag

1 Place the mouse pointer on the right edge of the column you want to resize. The mouse pointer changes to have four arrows.

2 Click and drag the column border to the left or right, depending on whether you want to make the column more narrow or widen the column.

3 The column is resized.

End

In Datasheet view, all columns in a table are the same size. You can, however, resize columns as needed. For example, if you cannot see the entire entry in a column, you can make the column wider. You can also make columns with shorter entries narrower so that you can see more columns onscreen.

Selecting Other Columns?
If, when you drag, you accidentally select additional columns instead of resizing the intended column, click the column first to select it. Then release the mouse button and commence with the dragging operation.

Resizing Row Height
You can use this same basic procedure to change a record's row height. Place the mouse pointer on the row's bottom borders and drag up or down to resize. When you resize one row, you resize all rows in the database table.

Rearranging Columns

Start

Click

Click and Drag

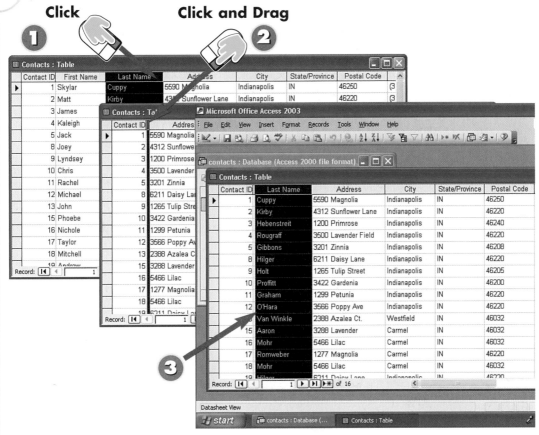

1. Select the column you want to move.

2. Drag the column to its new location. As you drag, you see a vertical line.

3. When the vertical line is in the desired location, release the mouse button. The column is moved.

End

If you want, you can change the order of the columns in your table. You might do this if you discover that another column order works better for data entry. Note, however, that changing the order of the columns in Datasheet view does not alter the structure of the table itself (to change that, see Part 4).

Selecting Other Columns?

TIP

If, when you drag, you accidentally select additional columns instead of moving the intended column, make sure that you click the column first to select it. Then release the mouse button and commence with the dragging operation.

Editing a Record

Start

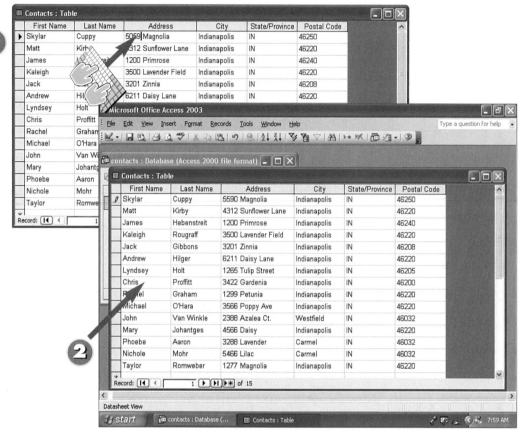

After you've displayed the record you want to change, click in the field you want to edit, and type a new entry or edit the existing one.

Click anywhere outside the current field to update the edited entry.

End

Part of keeping your database current is updating information as needed. People move. Phone numbers change. Data is entered incorrectly. In these and any other cases where you need to make a change, you can edit records.

Undoing a Change
You can open the **Edit** menu and choose **Undo** to undo a change you made in error.

Deleting a Record

Deleting a Record

Start

Click **2**

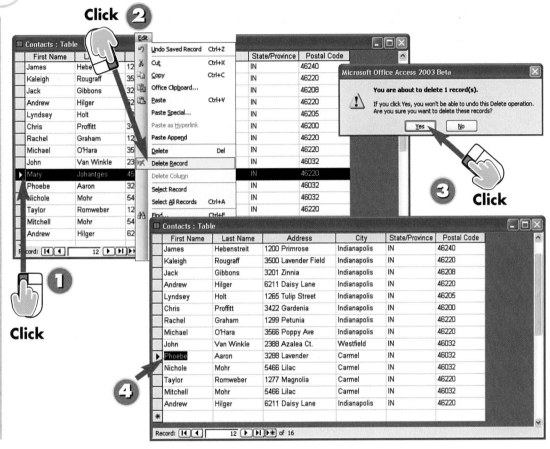

Click

Click

1

4

3

1 Select the record you want to delete.

2 Open the **Edit** menu and choose **Delete Record**.

3 Access prompts you to confirm the deletion. Click **Yes**.

4 The record is deleted.

End

INTRODUCTION

If you have a record in your table that is no longer valid, you can delete it. Deleting old records helps keep your data streamlined.

TIP

Deleting an Entry
You can delete a single entry within a field. To do so, select the entry and then press the **Delete** key on your keyboard.

CAUTION

You cannot undo a record deletion. Be absolutely certain that you want to delete the record before clicking **Yes** in step 3.

Copying an Entry

Start

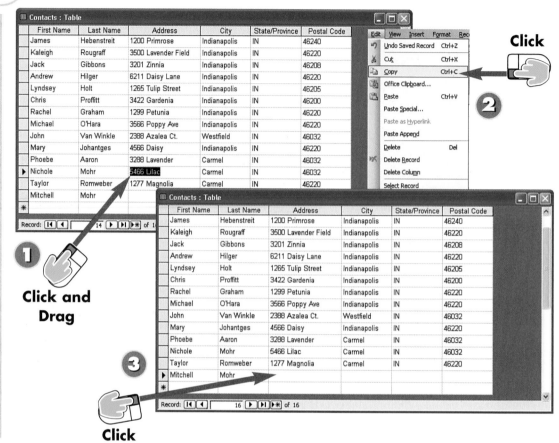

Click

Click and Drag

Click

1. Select the entry you want to copy.

2. Open the **Edit** menu and choose **Copy**.

3. Click in the field in which you want to paste the copied data.

Instead of retyping data that will appear in several records in your table, you can copy an entry (or partial entry) from one field to another. For example, you could copy the address from an existing record to a new record.

Using a Data-Entry Shortcut

If a field in a new record requires the same value as the entry in the row preceding it (for example, both records should contain **Indianapolis** in the **City** field), click in the field then press **Ctrl+'**. The entry will be duplicated in the new record, using the value from the row above it.

Click

4

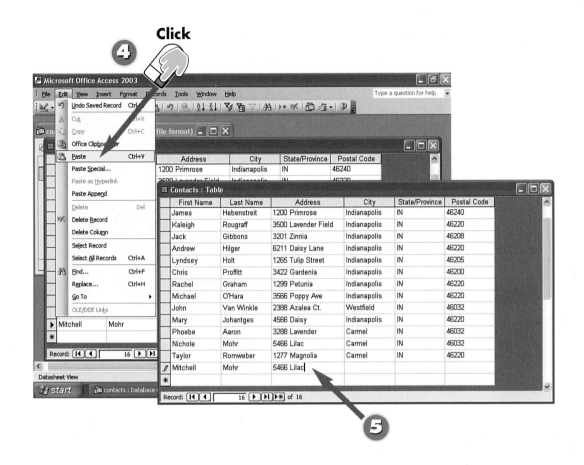

(4) Open the **Edit** menu and choose **Paste**.

(5) The copied data is pasted into the field.

End

Shortcuts
If you prefer, you can use the **Copy** and **Paste** toolbar buttons or the keyboard shortcut keys (**Ctrl+C** for copy and **Ctrl+V** for paste).

Moving an Entry
You use this same basic process to move, rather than copy, an entry from one location to another. Instead of opening the **Edit** menu and choosing **Copy**, use **Edit**, **Cut**.

Copying an Entire Record

Start

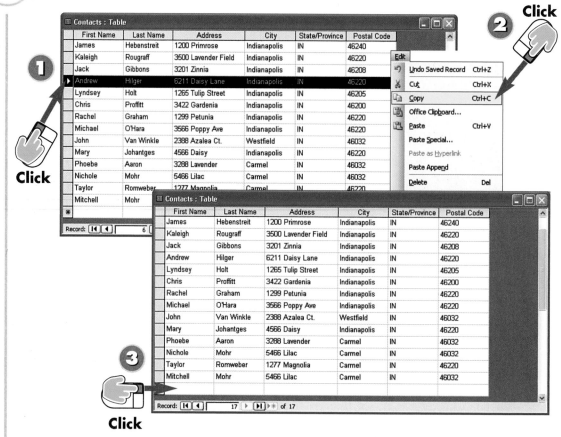

Click

Click

Click

1. Select the record you want to copy.

2. Open the **Edit** menu and choose **Copy**.

3. Click in the blank row at the bottom of the database table.

As another shortcut for entering similar records, you can copy an entire record. You can then edit any of the fields to create a unique record. For example, suppose that you are entering records for several individuals from the same company. Because most of the fields in the record will be the same—company name, company address, and so on—you could create one record, copy it, paste it into your table several times (once for each record you need to create), and then modify the fields in the new records as needed to make each one unique.

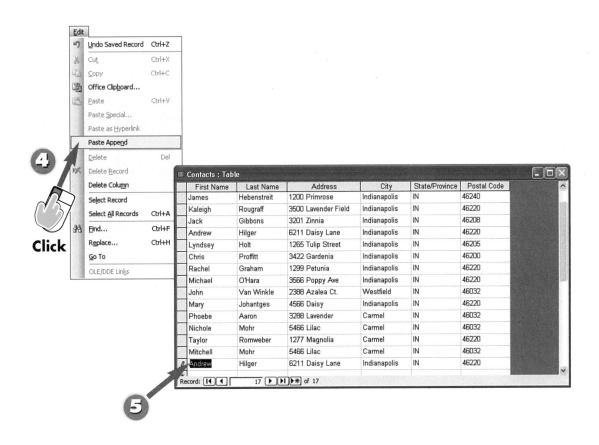

4 Open the **Edit** menu and choose **Paste Append**.

5 The copied record is pasted. Edit the record as needed.

End

Moving a Record

TIP
You use this same basic process to move, rather than copy, a record from one location to another. Instead of opening the **Edit** menu and choosing **Copy**, use **Edit**, **Cut**. Then move to the location where you want to place the record, open the **Edit** menu, and choose **Paste Append**.

Sorting Records in Datasheet View

Start

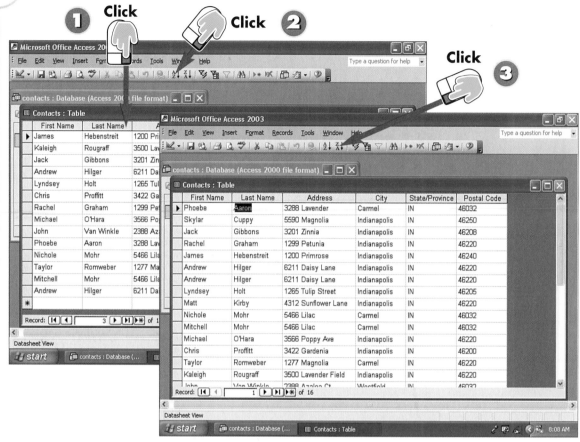

Click ①   **Click** ②   **Click** ③

① Click in the field, or column, on which you want to sort. For example, to sort your records by last name, click in the Last Name column.

② Click the **Sort Ascending** button in the Standard toolbar of the main Access window to sort in ascending order (that is, from A–Z) .

③ The records are sorted in ascending order (here by last name). Click the **Sort Descending** button to sort the records in descending order.

Access stores records in the database table in the order you enter them. Fortunately, you don't have to worry about creating a special order entry because you can easily sort records based on any of the fields in the table. For example, you can sort records in a table by last name, by state, or by any other field in the table. In addition, you can sort records in ascending or descending order.

Click

4

Contacts : Table						
First Name	Last Name	Address	City	State/Province	Postal Code	
▶ John	Van Winkle	2388 Azalea Ct.	Westfield	IN	46032	
Kaleigh	Rougraff	3500 Lavender Field	Indianapolis	IN	46220	
Taylor	Romweber	1277 Magnolia	Carmel	IN	46220	
Chris	Proffitt	3422 Gardenia	Indianapolis	IN	46200	
Michael	O'Hara	3566 Poppy Ave	Indianapolis	IN	46220	
Mitchell	Mohr	5466 Lilac	Carmel	IN	46032	
Nichole	Mohr	5466 Lilac	Carmel	IN	46032	
Matt	Kirby	4312 Sunflower Lane	Indianapolis	IN	46220	
Lyndsey	Holt	1265 Tulip Street	Indianapolis	IN	46205	
Andrew	Hilger	6211 Daisy Lane	Indianapolis	IN	46220	
Andrew	Hilger	6211 Daisy Lane	Indianapolis	IN	46220	
James	Hebenstreit	1200 Primrose	Indianapolis	IN	46240	
Rachel	Graham	1299 Petunia	Indianapolis	IN	46220	
Jack	Gibbons	3201 Zinnia	Indianapolis	IN	46208	
Skylar	Cuppy	5590 Magnolia	Indianapolis	IN	46250	
Phoebe	Aaron	3288 Lavender	Carmel	IN	46032	

Record: |◄ ◄ 1 ► ►I ►* of 16

4 The records are sorted in descending order.

End

HINT

Original Order

If you do want to be able to return to the original order entry, make sure that your table includes an AutoNumber field. You can then re-sort on this field to return to the original order.

TIP

Using Menu Commands

If you prefer, you can use menu commands to sort your records. To do so, click in the column by which you want to sort, open the **Records** menu, choose **Sort**, and then choose **Sort Ascending** or **Sort Descending**.

Finding Data

Start

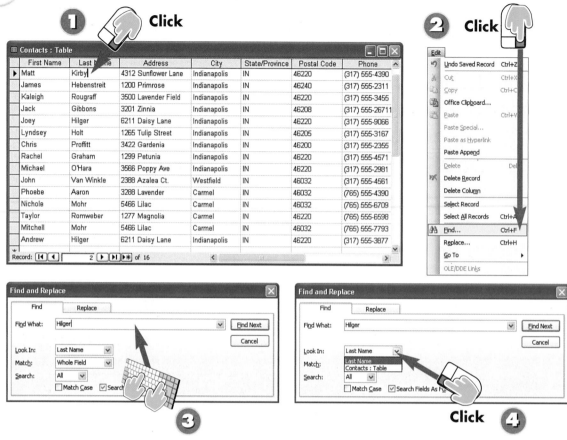

1. Click in the field, or column, on which you want to search. For example, to search by last name, click anywhere in the **Last Name** column.

2. Open the **Edit** menu and choose **Find**.

3. The Find and Replace dialog box opens with the Find tab displayed. In the **Find What** field, type the entry you want to find.

4. Optionally, to search the entire table rather than the field you chose in step 1, click the **down arrow** next to the **Look in** field and choose the table name from the list that appears.

In a large table, scanning through the records to find the one you want may be too time-consuming. Instead, *search* for the record you need. Access enables you to search any of the table's fields. For example, if you remember a client's first name but not his last, you can search for all matching first names.

Understanding Search Options

The various search options in the Find and Replace dialog box enable you to narrow your search. For example, suppose that you know that a customer's last name starts with **Str** but aren't sure what follows. You could type **Str** in the **Find What** field and then select **Start of Field** from the **Match** drop-down list. You can also specify that Access return only those entries that match the capitalization you typed. For example, if you type **Smith** in the **Find What** field, Access returns records that contain the entry **Smith**, but not **smith** or **SMITH**.

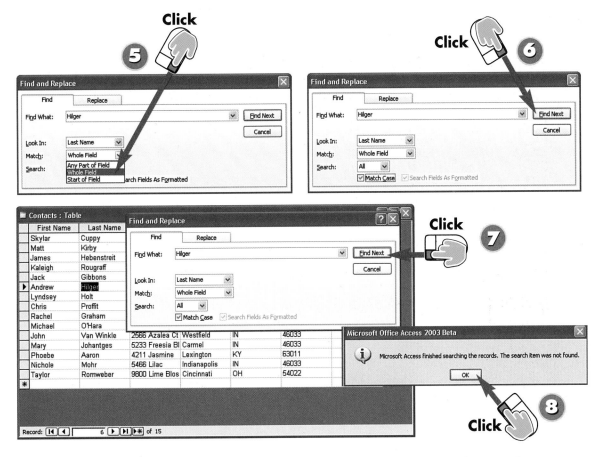

Click the down arrow next to the Match field and select **Whole Field**, **Any Part of Field**, or **Start of Field**.

Click the **Find Next** button.

Access locates and selects the record with the first matching entry. If this is not the record you need, click the **Find Next** button to find the next match and repeat as needed.

Access notifies you when no more matches are found. Click **OK**.

Moving the Dialog Box
You may need to move the Find and Replace dialog box to view the matches. Click and drag the dialog box's title bar to move it out of the way.

Closing Find and Replace
To close the Find and Replace dialog box, click the **Cancel** button.

Replacing Data

Start

Click ①

Click ②

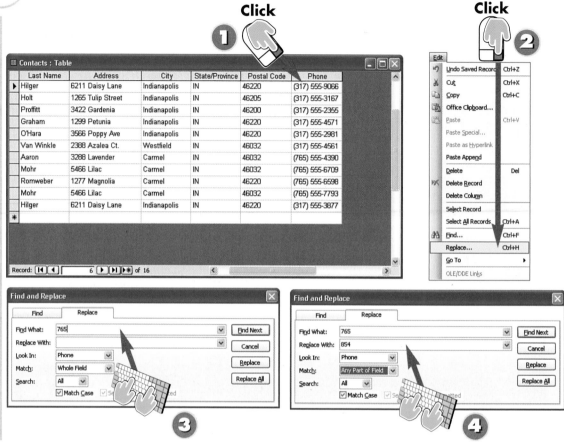

① Click anywhere in the field, or column, that contains the entries you want to replace.

② Open the **Edit** menu and choose **Replace**.

③ The Find and Replace dialog box opens with the Replace tab displayed. In the **Find What** field, type the entry you want to find.

④ In the **Replace With** field, type the entry to use as the replacement.

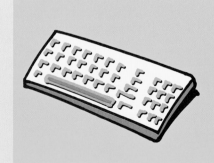

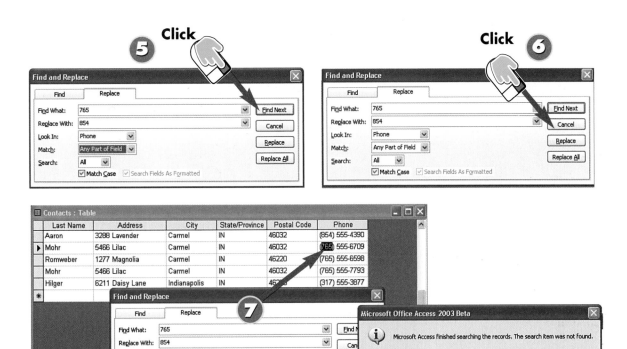

5 After you've made any necessary changes to the search options, click the **Find Next** button. (To learn more about the various search options, see the preceding task.)

6 Access locates and selects the record with the first matching entry. To replace it, click the **Replace** button.

7 The replacement is made. Access moves to the next match; continue making replacements as needed.

8 Access notifies you when no more matches are found. Click **OK**.

End

Skipping a Replacement

If Access locates a match that you do not want to replace, click the **Find Next** button. Access moves to the next match, where you can choose to skip or replace.

Making All Replacements

Click **Replace All** to make all the replacements. Before doing so, however, make sure that the Replace operation is working as you intended. Otherwise, you can wind up making replacements you didn't intend. For example, if you replace all instances of **form** with **report**, you can end up with words like **reportatted** instead of **formatted**.

Formatting the Datasheet

Start

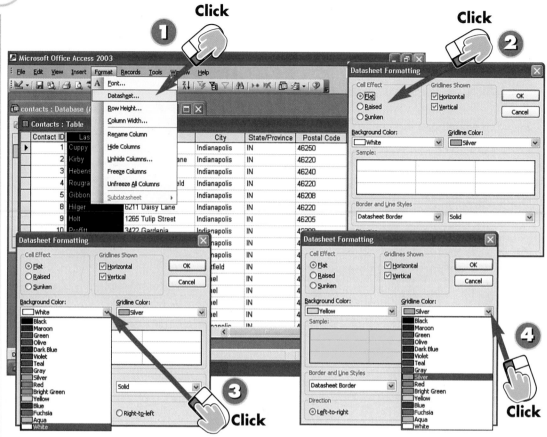

1 Open the **Format** menu and choose **Datasheet**.

2 The Datasheet Formatting dialog box opens. Choose **Flat**, **Raised**, or **Sunken** in the **Cell Effect** area to specify how cells in the datasheet should look.

3 To apply a background color to the datasheet (the default is white), click the **down arrow** next to the **Background Color** field and choose a color from the list that appears.

4 To change the color of the datasheet's gridlines, click the **down arrow** next to the **Gridline Color** field and choose a color from the list that appears.

If you do not like the plain appearance of the datasheet (that is, the view of the table you use for entering records), you can modify its look. For example, you can apply a cell effect, turn on or off gridlines, and use background colors. These changes affect only the open datasheet.

TIP

Hiding Gridlines
Gridlines appear in the datasheet by default. To turn them off, uncheck the **Horizontal** check box, the **Vertical** check box, or both in the **Gridlines Shown** area of the Datasheet Formatting dialog box. You might do this when printing the datasheet.

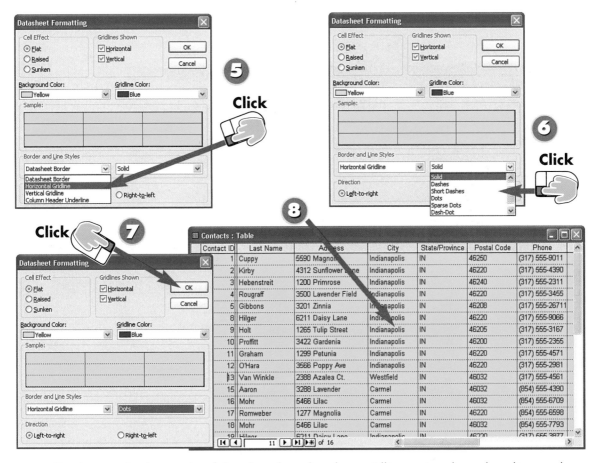

Click

Click

Click

To change the line style of the datasheet border, gridlines, or column heading underline, select the item to change from the leftmost drop-down list in the **Border and Line Styles** area.

Click the **down arrow** next to the rightmost field in the **Border and Line Styles** area and select a line style for the datasheet border, gridline, or column heading underline.

The Sample area of the Datasheet Formatting dialog box shows a preview of your changes. If you are satisfied with the datasheet's new appearance, click **OK**.

End

The datasheet is formatted with your selections.

Reversing the Column Order

To reverse the column order (putting the first column last and last column first), select the **Right-to-left** option button in the **Direction** area of the Datasheet Formatting dialog box.

Changing the Font

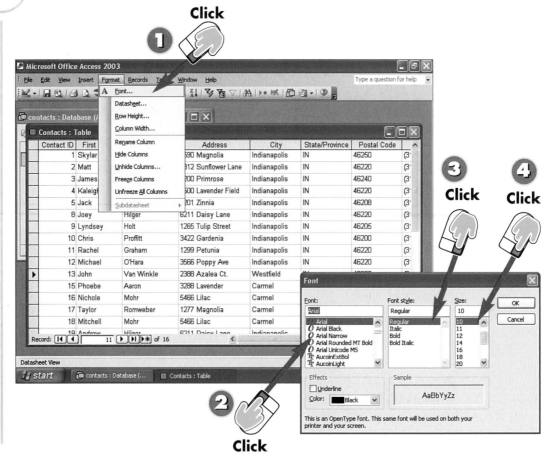

Click

Click

Click

Click

1. Open the **Format** menu and choose **Font**.

2. The Font dialog box opens. Click a font in the **Font** list. (You may need to click the scroll arrows to the right of the list to view all the available fonts.)

3. Click a font style (regular, bold, italic, or bold and italic) in the **Font style** list.

4. Click a font size in the **Size** list.

Access uses Arial as the default font for entries. If you prefer a different typeface, you can change the font. You can also change the selected font's size and style.

Font Sizes

Fonts are measured in *points*, and there are 72 points to an inch. Therefore, the larger the point size, the bigger the font's text size.

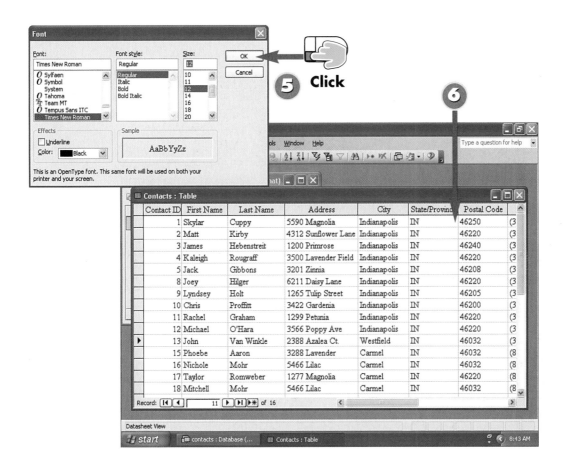

5 The Sample of the Font dialog box shows a preview of your changes. If you are satisfied with your font choices, click **OK** to make the changes.

6 The datasheet is formatted using your font selections.

End

Undo Command Doesn't Work
The **Edit, Undo** command will not undo this formatting change. If you want to undo the change, follow the steps in this task, selecting the original font, style, and size.

Underlining
You can choose to underline your entries. To do so, check the **Underline** check box in the Effects area of the Font dialog box. Then select an underline color from the **Color** drop-down list.

Checking Spelling

Start

Click

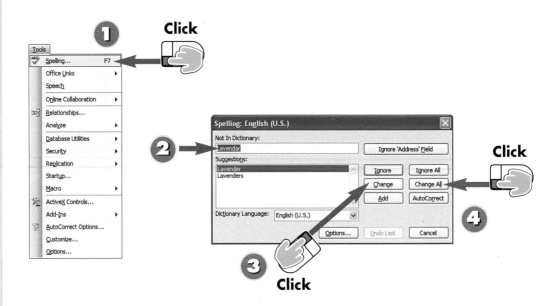

Click

Click

1. Open the **Tools** menu and choose **Spelling** to open the Spelling dialog box.

2. When Access finds a word that does not appear in its dictionary, the word appears in the **Not In Dictionary** field, with suggested corrections in the **Suggestions** area.

3. If the word is, in fact, misspelled and the correct spelling is listed, click the correct spelling to select it, and click the **Change** button to change just this instance of the word.

4. To change all instances of the misspelled word, click the correct spelling in the **Suggestions** list and then click the **Change All** button.

Because a database table is likely to include names and other proper nouns that are probably not in the speller's dictionary, you may find that checking spelling isn't as useful in this program as it is in, say, Word. Still, you can and should check the spelling of your entries to catch any mistakes.

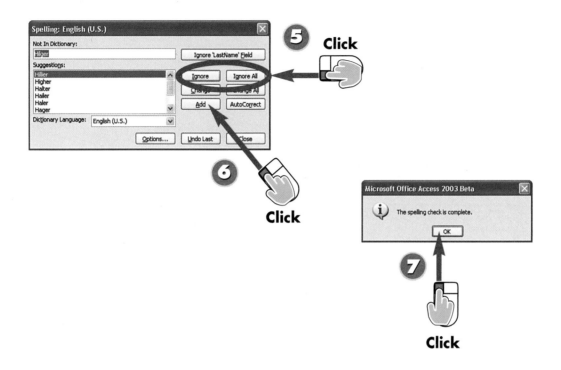

Click

Click

Click

⑤ If Access incorrectly flags a word as a misspelling, you can opt to ignore the flag. Click **Ignore** to skip just this instance, or **Ignore All** to skip all instances.

⑥ If Access incorrectly flags a word as a misspelling, and it's one you use often, click the **Add** button to add the word to the dictionary that Access uses to check your spelling.

⑦ Access flags the next word not found in its dictionary. Continue making selections for each of the flagged words. Access notifies you when the spell check is complete; click **OK**.

End

Skipping a Field

To speed the spell-check process, you can have Access ignore the entries in a particular field. To do so, click the **Ignore Field** button. (The exact name of the button varies depending on what field is flagged. For example, if you wanted to ignore entries in the LastName field, you'd click the Ignore LastName Field button.)

Using AutoCorrect
If you often misspell a particular word, you can configure Access to always correct it automatically by selecting the correct spelling in the **Suggestions** list and then clicking the **AutoCorrect** button.

Previewing and Printing a Table

Start

Click ❶

Click ❷

Click ❸

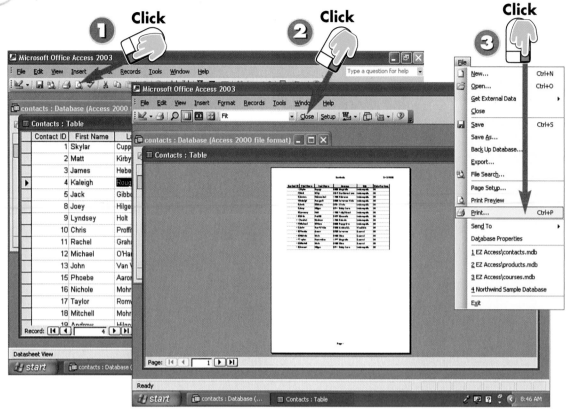

❶ Click the **Print Preview** button on the Standard toolbar in Access's main window.

❷ The table is displayed in Print Preview mode, enabling you to see how the printed data will look. Click the **Close** button to return to Datasheet view.

❸ To print the table, open the **File** menu and choose **Print**.

INTRODUCTION

For a nice presentation of your data, you can create a report (see Part 7). For a quick printout of your table, however, you can print directly from Datasheet view. The table is printed in the gridlike format, as it appears onscreen. Column headings (field names) are included. You can preview the printout before printing.

Preview Buttons

When you are previewing the table, you can use the toolbar buttons to zoom in, display multiple-page views, and print.

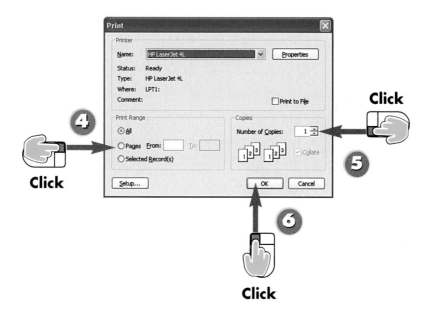

Click

Click

Click

④ The Print dialog box opens. To print a page range, select the range in the **Page Range** area.

⑤ To print more than one copy of the table, enter the number of copies to print in the **Number of Copies** field.

⑥ Click **OK**. The database table is printed.

End

Editing a Database's Table Structure

No doubt you spent a lot of time planning your database, mapping out its structure, before you created it. Even the most thorough planners, however, may discover that their databases require a few changes. For example, you may find that you need to add new fields or remove existing ones. You can also make changes to your database to make data entry easier, such as setting default values in fields. You can even make changes to your database to ensure that entries are valid, such as requiring a unique entry in an ID field. That's the focus of this part: making changes to enhance your database's usability.

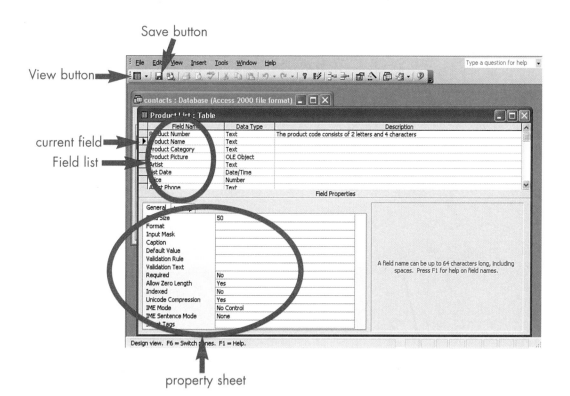

Save button

View button

current field

Field list

property sheet

Viewing Field Properties

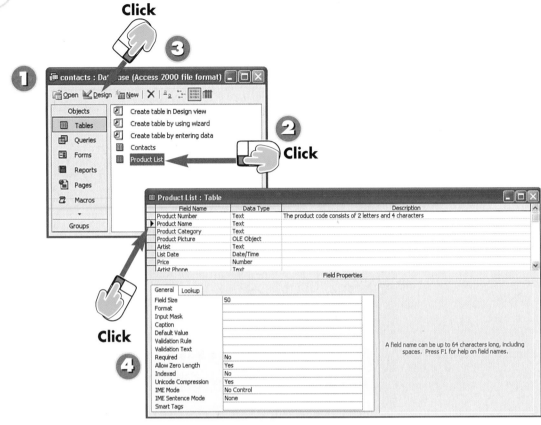

1 Open the database that contains the table you want to modify.

2 Click the table to select it.

3 Click the **Design** button to open the table in Design view.

4 Click a field to view its properties. In this example, **Product Name**, a text field, is selected.

Each field in a table has several identifying qualities, such as a name, a size, a data type, and so on. These elements are called the field's properties and are displayed in the property sheet, found in the lower half of the Access window in Design view. In addition to the common properties that you learned about when you created a table, fields have other properties that you can display and modify such as display formats.

INTRODUCTION

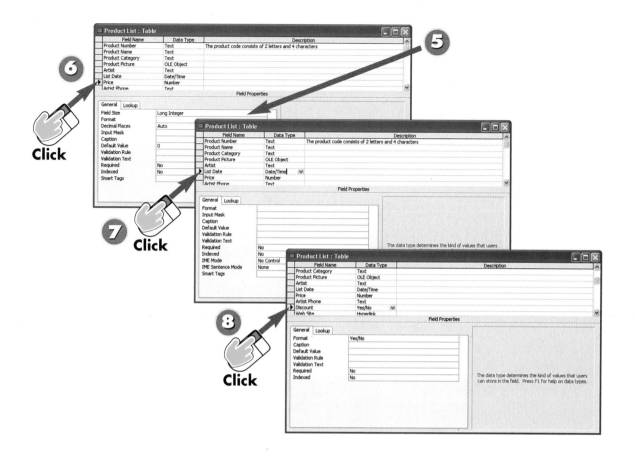

5 The property sheet, found in the bottom part of the window, displays the various properties for the selected text field.

6 Click another field to view its properties. In this example, **Price**, a Number field, is selected; notice that the properties vary depending on the field type.

7 Click a field with **Date/Time** listed as the data type to see the available properties for a Date/Time field.

8 Click a field with **Yes/No** listed as the data type to see the available properties for a Yes/No field.

End

Viewing a Property Description
This book discusses only those field properties most commonly used in Access. For information about other field properties, click in the appropriate property field and view the description displayed on the right side of the window. You can also consult online help using the Access Help menu.

Saving Your Database
Remember that when you make changes to your database structure, you need to save the database. To do so, click the **Save** button on the Standard toolbar found in the main Access window.

Using Display Formats

Start

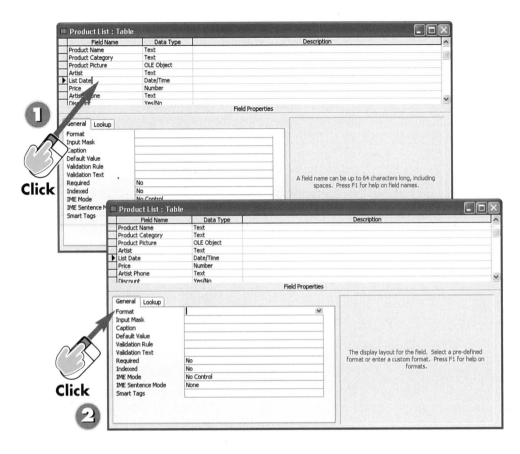

Click ①

Click ②

---

① After you've opened the table you want to change in Design view, click in the field whose display format you want to modify (in this example, the **List Date** field).

② In the property sheet, click in the **Format** field. A down arrow appears to the right of the field.

Access enables you to select a predesigned format for the entries in your table. For example, you can select one format to display numbers in a currency format ($19.99), or another to display numbers as a percentage (10%). You can also select a variety of date and time formats.

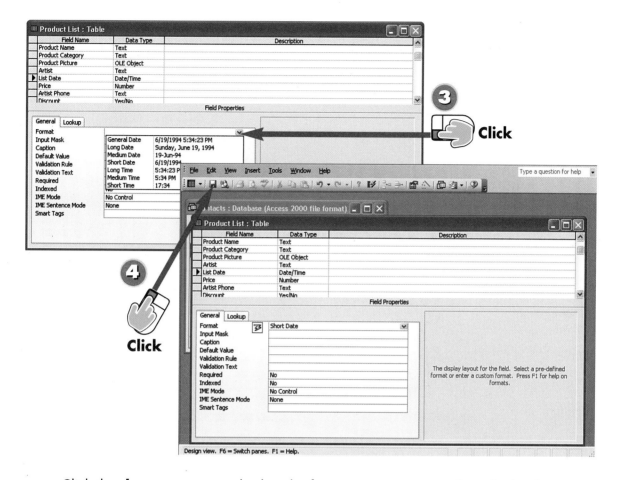

Click the **down arrow** and select the format you want to use from the list that
appears. Here, date and time formats are available, because the field selected in
step 1 is a Date/Time field.

The new format is selected. Click the **Save** button on the Standard toolbar found in
the main Access window to save this change to the database table.

Changing to Design View
You can change to Design view
from within Datasheet view by
clicking the View button on the
Standard toolbar in the main
Access window.

Adding Decimal Places
For Number fields, you can set
the number of decimal places
displayed by typing a value in
the **Decimal Places** field in
the property sheet.

Using an Input Mask

Start

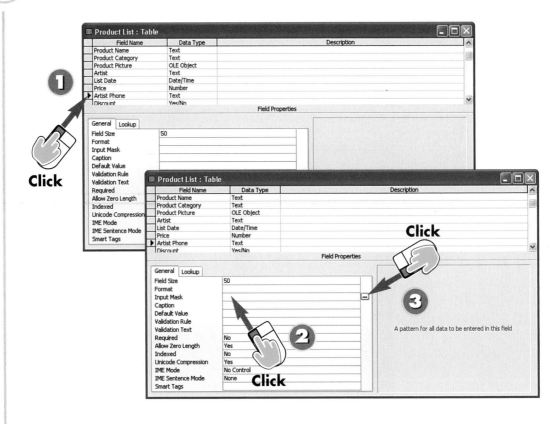

Click

Click

Click

1 After you've opened the table you want to change in Design view, click in the field to which you want to apply an input mask (in this example, the **Artist Phone** field).

2 In the property sheet, click in the **Input Mask** field. A button featuring an ellipsis appears to the right of the field.

3 Click the **ellipsis** button.

INTRODUCTION

One way to simplify data entry is to use an *input mask*. Input masks are similar to the display formats discussed in the preceding task, but input masks are displayed before data is entered in a field and are meant to indicate to the person entering data what an appropriate entry for the field might be. For example, you might use an input mask containing parentheses and a dash for a phone number field so that entries appear as follows: (555) 555-1212. You can also select input masks for other common fields such as ones for social-security numbers and ZIP codes.

Click

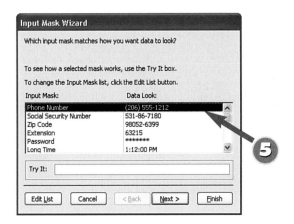

4 Access prompts you to save the database before continuing. Click **Yes**.

5 Access launches the Input Mask Wizard; the first screen displays a list of available input masks. Select the input mask you want to apply to this field.

Customizing Input Masks

TIP

Access includes several common input masks, but you can create your own. For instance, you may want to set up a mask for a product number. To do so, choose a similar mask from the Input Mask list found in the first screen of the Input Mask Wizard, but click **Edit List** rather than **Next**. Create the new entry, using Access's help system for specific instructions.

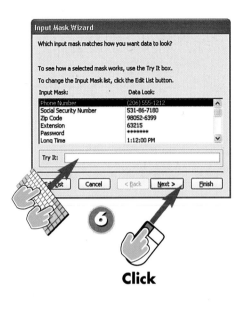

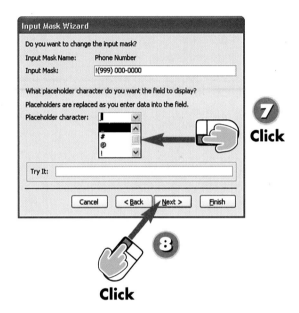

Click

Click

Click

⑥ To see how the input mask looks, type a phone number in the **Try It** text box. If you're satisfied, click **Next** to continue.

⑦ The next screen of the wizard appears. In the **Placeholder character** list, click the character you want Access to display as a placeholder in the input mask.

⑧ Click **Next**.

Validating Data with Input Masks

Because input masks require that a certain number of characters be entered, they can serve an important role in data validation. If someone enters the wrong number of characters in an input-mask field by accident, Access displays an error message noting that fact.

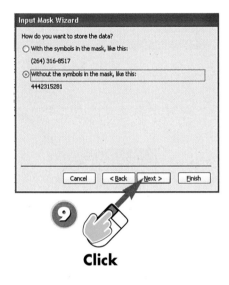

Click

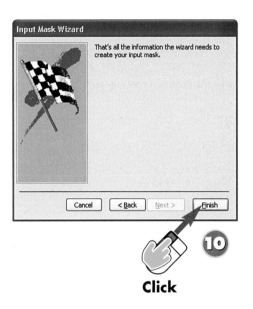

Click

9 The Input Mask Wizard asks you how you want to store the data that is entered — with or without the symbols used in the input mask. Make your selection and click **Next**.

10 Click **Finish**.

Backing Up

If necessary, you can click the **Back** button found in the various Input Mask Wizard screens to go back a step and modify an earlier selection.

PART 4

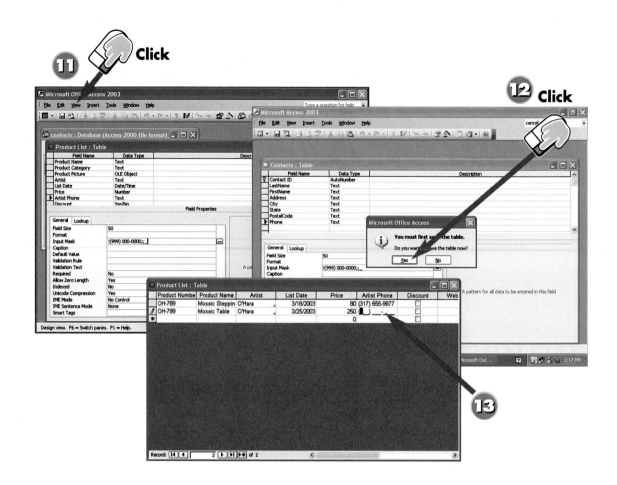

11 The new input mask is added to the property sheet. Click the **View** toolbar button to toggle to Datasheet view.

12 Before it changes to Datasheet view, Access prompts you to save the changes to the table; click **Yes** to do so.

13 Any blank fields for this field contain the selected input mask and placeholders. Here, you type only the digits in the phone number, not the parentheses around the area code or the dash within the number.

End

Placeholders
Placeholders are the characters that appear in the datasheet when you are entering data in the input mask field.

Adding a Field Caption

Start

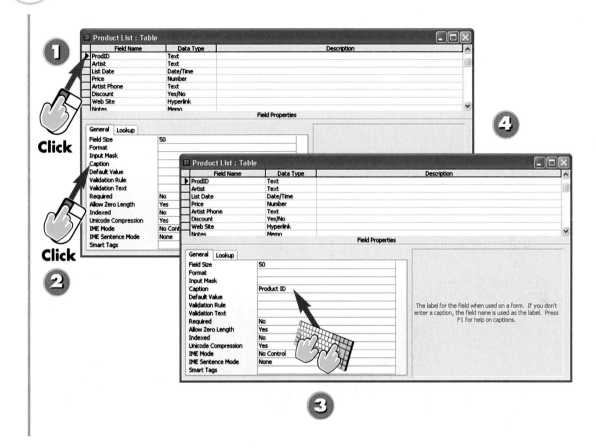

Click

Click

---

1 After you've opened the table you want to change in Design view, click in the field to which you want to add a caption (in this example, the **ProdID** field).

2 In the property sheet, click in the **Caption** field.

3 Type the caption.

4 The caption is now included as part of the database table design. Click the **Save** button on the Standard toolbar in the main Access window to save changes to the table.

End

INTRODUCTION

Adding captions to your field can greatly aid users entering data into your database. You won't notice the change in Datasheet view, but when you create a form (covered in the next part), the caption you add here will be used as the label for the field (rather than the field name). For example, suppose that you have a field titled **LName**. You can create a caption that says **Last Name** so that the form's label for that field is easier to understand.

TIP

Forget to Save?
If you try to move out of a property field without saving, Access prompts you to save your changes. Click the **Yes** button to save the database table changes.

Entering a Default Value

Start

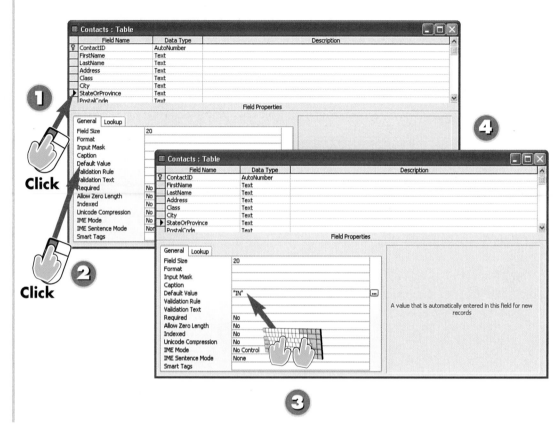

Click

Click

1 After you've opened the table you want to change in Design view, click in the field for which you want to enter a default value (in this example, the **StateOrProvince** field).

2 In the property sheet, click in the **Default Value** field.

3 Type the default value in quotation marks (in this example, **"IN"** is entered).

4 The default value is now included as part of the database table design. Click the **Save** button on the Standard toolbar in the main Access window to save change the table.

End

If you commonly enter the same value in a field, you can set a default value. For example, suppose that most of your business is local. In that case, you could enter your state as the default state if your table contains a StateOrProvince field or something similar. That way, you won't have to type the state each time you create a new record. You can always override the default when needed.

Existing Data

Existing entries are not affected by this change. Only new records that you create will use the default value. Remember, however, that you can always override the default value by typing a different entry.

Requiring an Entry

Start

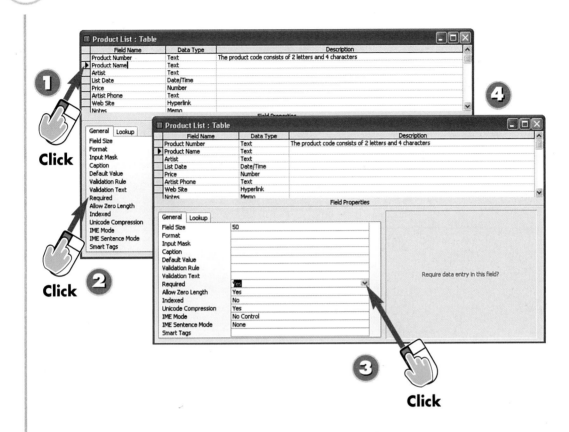

Click 1

Click 2

Click 3

4

1. After you've opened the table you want to change in Design view, click in the field for which you want to require an entry (in this example, the **Product Name** field).

2. In the property sheet, click in the **Required** field. A down arrow appears to the right of the field.

3. Click the **down arrow** and select **Yes** from the list that appears.

4. This field now requires an entry. Click the **Save** button on the Standard toolbar in the main Access window to save changes to the table.

End

INTRODUCTION

For some fields, you may want to make sure that data is entered. For example, suppose that you have a product database table and that all products must have an ID. You can make the field that contains this value a required field so that the user is prompted to enter a value.

TIP

Handling Error Messages
Access lets you move out of the required field without typing an entry, but when you move out of the record containing the required field, you'll see an error message that names the required field. Click **OK**, complete the required field, and add the record.

Indexing a Field

Start

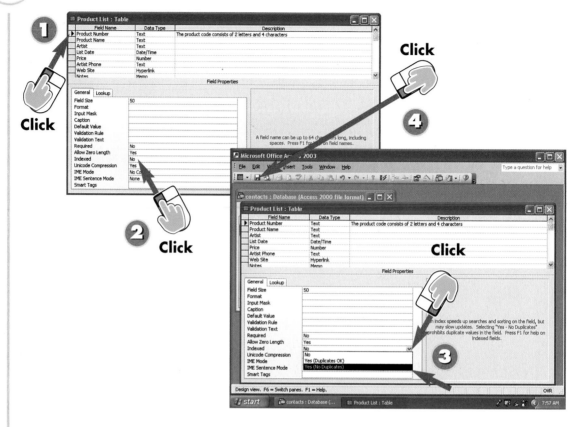

1 After you've opened the table you want to change in Design view, click in the field you want to index (in this example, the **Product Number** field).

2 In the property sheet, click in the **Indexed** field. A down arrow appears to the right of the field.

3 Click the **down arrow** and, in the list that appears, choose **Yes (Duplicates OK)** or **No (No Duplicates)** depending on your needs.

4 This field now will be indexed and may require a unique entry, depending on your selection. Click the **Save** button on the Standard toolbar to save changes to the table.

INTRODUCTION

In addition to using the primary key, you can create indexed fields to speed sorting and searches. Because indexing fields slows down updates, however, you should do so only on fields on which you often search or sort. When you specify that a field be indexed, you can also specify that the field contain a unique entry (that is, no duplicates). This is helpful for fields containing values that should be unique, such as a field containing a product ID. It wouldn't be necessary, however, for a field that contains last names because numerous people referenced in a database could have the same last name.

TIP

Entering Duplicate Values by Mistake
If you try to create a new record with a duplicate entry in an indexed field that doesn't accept duplicate values, you'll see an error message. Click **OK** and change the value in the indexed field to a unique entry.

Applying a Smart Tag

Start

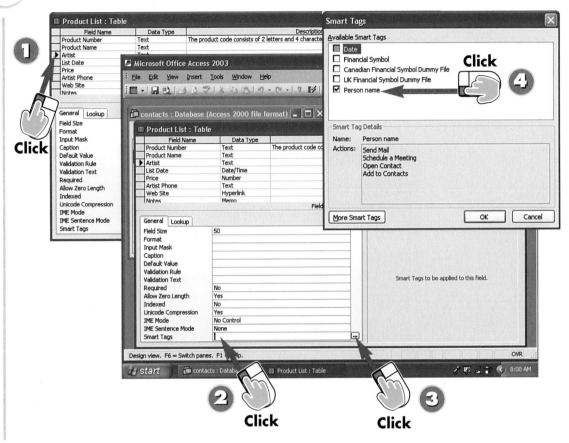

1 After you've opened the table you want to change in Design view, click in the field to which you want to apply a Smart Tag (in this example, the **Artist** field).

2 In the property sheet, click in the **Smart Tags** field. A button featuring an ellipsis appears to the right of the field.

3 Click the **ellipsis** button.

4 The Smart Tags dialog box opens. In the **Available Smart Tags** list, click the check box next to the type of Smart Tag you want to apply (in this example, **Person Name**) and click **OK**.

INTRODUCTION

One new feature of Office 2003 is Smart Tags, which enables you to use data from several applications at once. In many Office 2003 applications, Smart Tags appear when you complete an action that commonly occurs in conjunction with another action. For example, if you type a person's name, a Smart Tag appears; you can click it to select any number of options, such as sending an email, scheduling a meeting, and so on. In this task, you'll learn how to add Smart Tags to your database so that users can take advantage of the flexibility they offer.

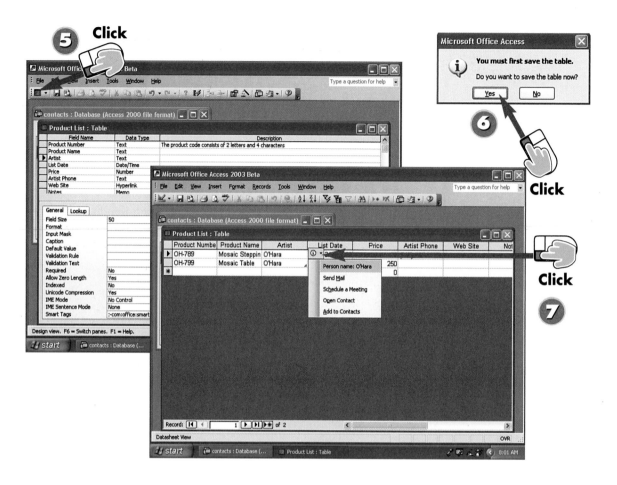

5 Click the **View** button on the Standard toolbar in the main Access window to toggle to Datasheet view.

6 Before it changes to Datasheet view, Access prompts you to save the changes to the table; click **Yes** to do so.

7 When you click the field in the table to which the Smart Tag was applied, a Smart Tag appears; click the **down arrow** to display the list of available actions.

End

Actions Vary
The Smart Tag's available actions vary depending on the type of Smart Tag you select in the Smart Tags dialog box (refer to step 4). Common data table field Smart Tags include Date, Financial Symbols (in various styles), and Person Name.

Displaying Additional Smart Tags
To view other available Smart Tags, click the **More Smart Tags** button in the Smart Tags dialog box.

Creating a Yes/No Field

Start

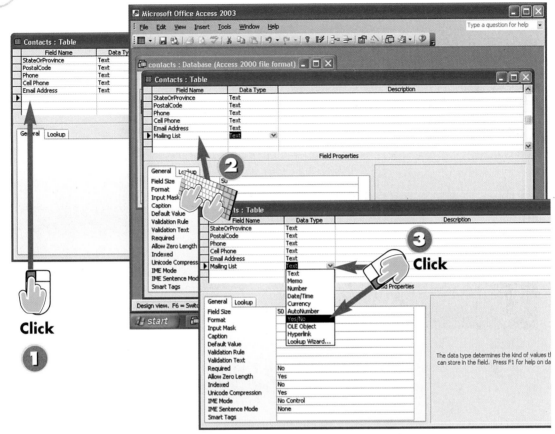

Click
1

1. After you've opened the table you want to change in Design view, click in the first empty row or insert a new row.

2. Type a name for the field (in this example, **Mailing List)** and press **Tab** to move the insertion point to the Data Type column.

3. Click the **down arrow** that appears in the Data Type column and click the **Yes/No** option in the list that appears.

INTRODUCTION

In Part 2, you learned how to create a table, but not about all the different types of fields you can add to a table. One such field type is the Yes/No field, useful for situations in which there are only two possible valid entries for a field: yes or no, true or false, or on or off. For example, you might use a Yes/No field to indicate whether a customer wants to be on a mailing list. You can add this type of field when you first create your table or later (as covered here).

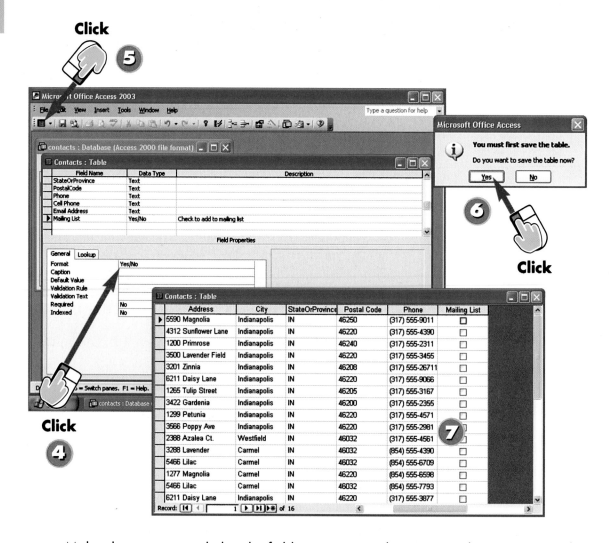

Click 5

Click 6

Click 4

Click 7

<table>
<tr><td>4</td><td>Make changes as needed to the field properties in the property sheet. For example, change the Format property from Yes/No to True/False or On/Off.</td></tr>
</table>

4 Make changes as needed to the field properties in the property sheet. For example, change the **Format** property from Yes/No to True/False or On/Off.

5 Click the **View** button on the Standard toolbar in the main Access window to toggle to Datasheet view.

6 Before it changes to Datasheet view, Access prompts you to save the changes to the table; click **Yes** to do so.

7 The Yes/No field is added. Here it is formatted as a check box; click the check box to select it for **Yes**, or leave it blank for **No**.

End

Yes/No Field Displays
To change how a Yes/No field is displayed in the Datasheet and forms, click the Lookup tab in the property sheet, open the Display Control drop-down list, and choose **Check Box**, **Text Box**, or **Combo Box**.

Creating a Hyperlink Field

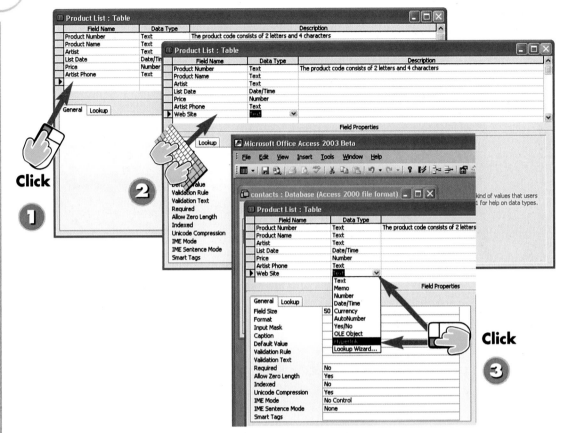

Click
1

2

Click
3

---

1 After you've opened the table you want to change in Design view, click in the first empty row or insert a new row.

2 Type a name for the field (in this example, **Web Site**) and press **Tab** to move the insertion point to the Data Type column.

3 Click the **down arrow** that appears in the Data Type column and click the **Hyperlink** option in the list that appears.

INTRODUCTION

If you need to store email addresses or Web site addresses in a field, select the Hyperlink data type. With a Hyperlink field, users can either type the address or open the Insert menu and choose Hyperlink to complete the entry for that field. Entries are formatted as links and work just like regular hyperlinks. That is, if the field contains an email address, you can click it to create a new email message addressed accordingly; if it contains a Web site address, you can click it to go to that Web site.

TIP

Inserting a New Row
You don't have to add a new field at the bottom of a table. You can insert a new row anywhere you want. To insert a row, select the field before which you want the new field to be inserted, open the **Insert** menu, and choose **Rows**.

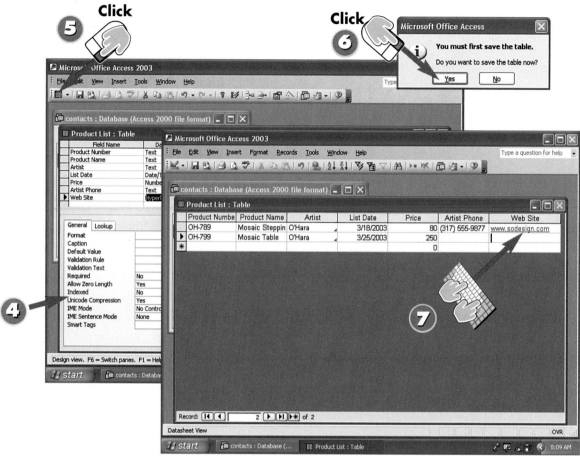

4️⃣ Make changes as needed to the field properties in the property sheet.

5️⃣ Click the **View** button on the Standard toolbar in the main Access window to toggle to Datasheet view.

6️⃣ Before it changes to Datasheet view, Access prompts you to save the changes to the table; click **Yes** to do so.

7️⃣ Enter a Web-site address or email address by typing it in the field or by opening the **Insert** menu, choosing **Hyperlink**, and selecting the hyper-link from the dialog box that appears.

End

Using the Insert, Hyperlink Command
As mentioned, you can open the **Insert** menu and choose the **Hyperlink** command to insert a link into a Hyperlink field. With this command, you can select to create a link to a Web page, to another object (such as a query) within the database, or to an email address.

Creating a Memo Field

Start

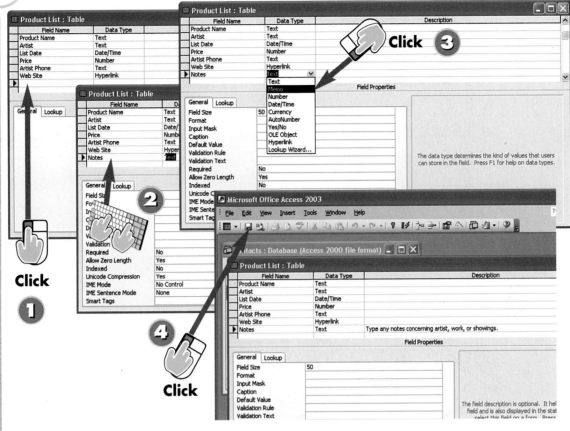

Click 3

1 After you've opened the table you want to change in Design view, click in the first empty row or insert a new row.

2 Type a name for the field (in this example, **Notes**) and press **Tab**.

3 Click the **down arrow** that appears in the Data Type column and click the **Memo** option in the list that appears.

4 Press **Tab** and type a description for the field if necessary. Click the **Save** button on the Standard toolbar in the main Access window to save changes to the table.

End

Creating an Object Field

Start

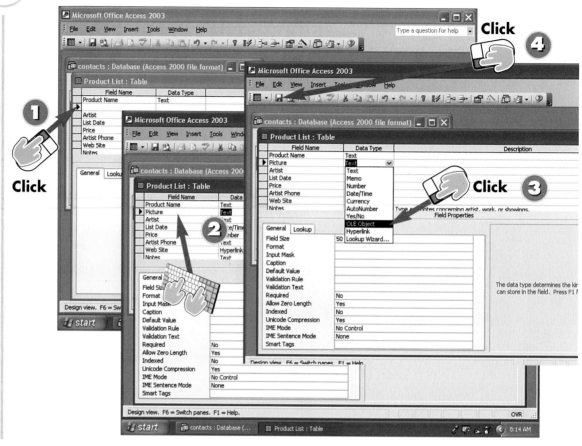

Click

Click

Click

1. After you've opened the table you want to change in Design view, click in the first empty row or insert a new row (shown here).

2. Type a name for the field (in this example, **Picture**) and press **Tab**.

3. Click the **down arrow** that appears in the Data Type column and click the **OLE Object** option in the list that appears.

4. Click the **Save** button to save the table design.

End

In addition to storing text, numbers, and links, you can also store *objects*, such as pictures, worksheets, sounds, and so on, in your database. For example, you might want to include a picture of each product in a product database table. You aren't limited to pictures, however; you can include a worksheet, Word document, sounds, and other file types.

TIP

Linking OLE Objects
When you insert an object, it is embedded in the database file, separate from the original file. You can, however, set up the OLE object so that the database object is linked to the original file. To do so, click the **Link** check box when inserting the file. When the files are linked, if you update the original file, the file in the database table is updated as well. Consult online help for more information on linking data from other programs to an Access table.

Adding an Entry to an Object Field

Start

Click 1

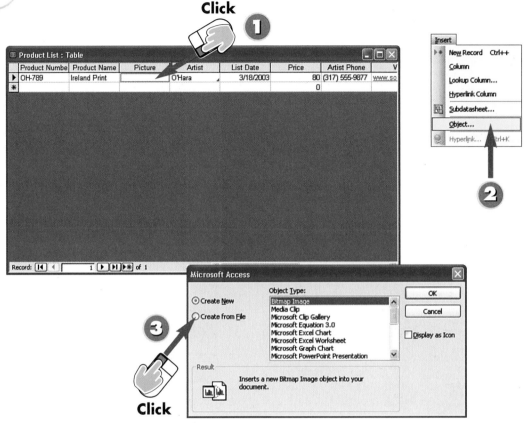

1. In Datasheet view, click in the field in which you want to insert the object.

2. Open the **Insert** menu and choose **Object**.

3. Click the **Create from File** option button to select an existing file to insert into the field.

Entering an OLE object in a database is not the same as typing text or numbers. Instead, you open the **Insert** menu and choose the **Object** command. You can then select the type of object and the object file to insert.

TIP

Creating a File On-the-Fly
Instead of inserting an existing file, you can also create a new file and insert it. To do so, click **Create New** in the dialog box shown in step 3, click the type of object you want to insert in the **Object Type**, and then click **OK**. Then, create the new object as directed.

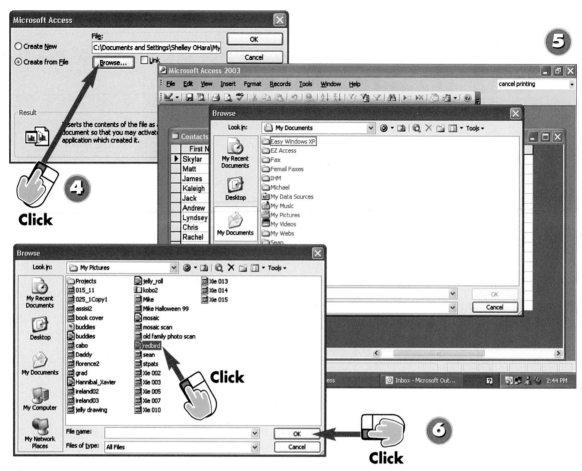

④ You see the Browse dialog box. Click the **Browse** button to select the file to insert.

⑤ Navigate to the drive and folder that contain the file.

⑥ Click the file you want to insert and click **OK**.

Changing Folders
You can use the Look in drop-down list, the Places bar or the Up One Level button to view the other folders.

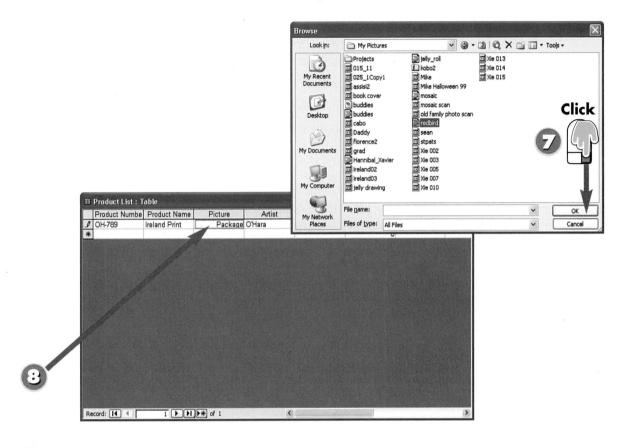

7 The file's name is listed in the dialog box; click **OK**.

8 The object is inserted in the field.

End

Displaying an Icon

If you want, you can display an icon that represents the inserted object rather than the object itself in the data table. To do so, check the **Display as Icon** check box.

Creating and Using Forms

When you enter data into a table using Datasheet view, you see a list of all the columns and rows[md]that is, all the records—in the table. Rather than view this information in list form, you can create a form that displays one record at a time. That way, you can concentrate on entering, editing, or reviewing a single record. Alternatively, you can use a form layout similar to the columns and rows of records you see in Datasheet view, but with a nicer appearance.

Like options for creating tables, Access provides multiple methods for creating a form: using AutoForms, using a wizard, and building one from scratch. This part covers how to create a form using a wizard, how to make changes to the form's design, and how to use the form to enter data. Because building a form from scratch takes some practice, use the simpler methods first and then experiment on your own, using Access's help system, if you need to create a form from scratch.

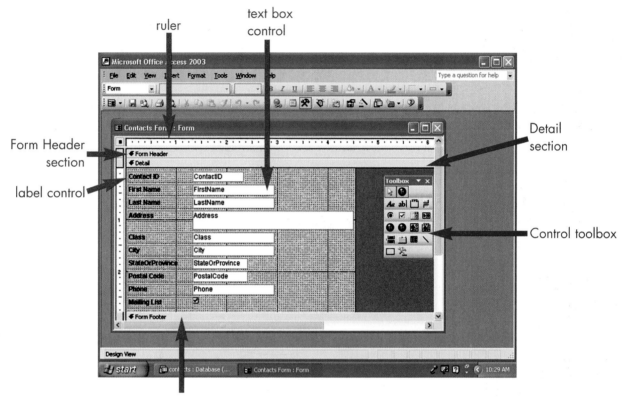

ruler

text box control

Detail section

Form Header section

label control

Control toolbox

Form Footer section

Creating a Form Using an AutoForm

Start

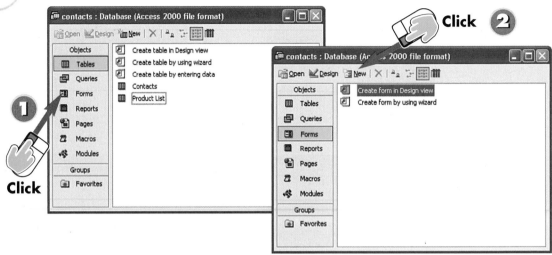

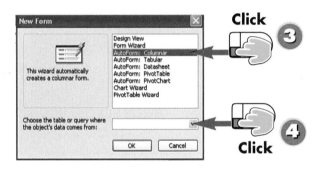

Click **2**

Click **3**

Click **4**

① After you open the database for which you want to create a form, click the **Forms** option in the Objects bar.

② Click the **New** button in the database window's toolbar.

③ The New Form dialog box opens. Click one of the available AutoForms to select it. A description of the selected AutoForm appears in the left side of the dialog box.

④ Click the **down arrow** next to the **Choose the table or query where the object's data comes from** field.

INTRODUCTION

Access 2003 features several AutoForms, which are, essentially, predesigned forms set up in typical form layouts. For example, there's a columnar AutoForm, a tabular AutoForm, and a Datasheet AutoForm. You can use these AutoForms to create a new form for a particular table; the AutoForm includes all the fields in that table.

TIP

Clicking the Forms Object
You must click the Forms option in the Objects bar to see the available commands and options for creating forms. If another object type is selected, you'll see commands for that type of object.

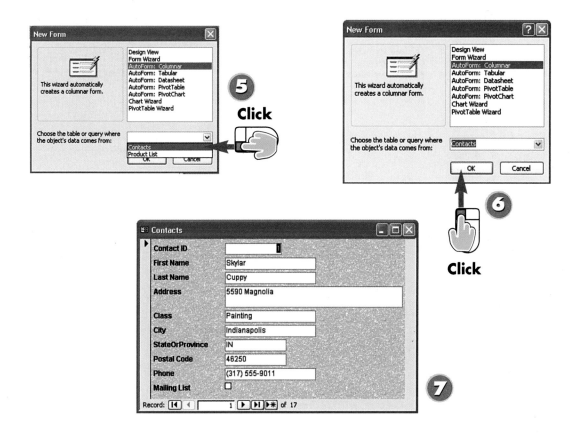

5 In the list that appears, click the table on which the form will be based.

6 Click **OK**.

7 Access creates the form (here, a columnar AutoForm) and displays the first record in the selected table in the form.

End

Creating a Form Using a Wizard

Start

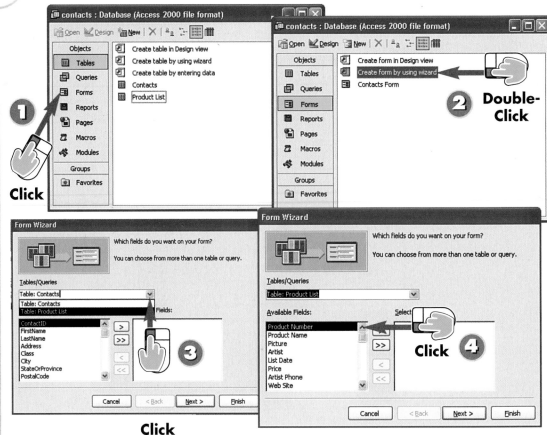

Click

Double-Click

Click

Click

1 After you open the database for which you want to create a form, click the **Forms** option in the Objects bar.

2 Double-click the **Create form by using wizard** option.

3 The Form Wizard starts. Click the down arrow next to the **Tables/Queries** field and select the table on which you want to base the form from the list that appears.

4 The **Available Fields** list catalogs all the fields in the selected table. Click the first field you want to appear in the form.

AutoForms are great if you want your form to include all the available fields in the selected table in the order they appear in the table. If, however, you want your form to include only certain fields, or to include fields in a different order, you'll want to use Access's Form Wizard to create your form. The wizard enables you to select only those fields you want and to place them in any order you choose.

Selecting Fields
You do not have to select all the fields in your table. Keep in mind, though, that when you add a new record using a form, the fields that were not included in the form will be blank in those records.

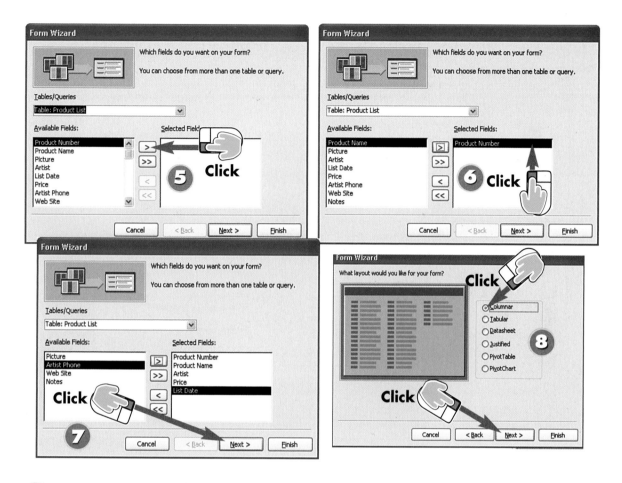

5 Click the **Add** button (it's the one with a single right-pointing arrow on it).

6 The field is added to the Selected Fields list. Continue selecting and adding fields until all the necessary fields appear in the Selected Fields list.

7 When you finish selecting the fields you want to appear in your form, click the **Next** button.

8 The Form Wizard displays a list of available layouts for your form. Click a layout to preview it in the left side of the dialog box. When you find a layout you like, click **Next**.

Adding and Removing Fields
If you want to include all available fields in your form, click the button that contains two right-pointing arrows. To remove a field from the Selected Fields list, select it and click the left-pointing arrow button.

Listing Fields
The fields are listed in the order you add them. If you prefer a particular order, simply add the fields in the order you want.

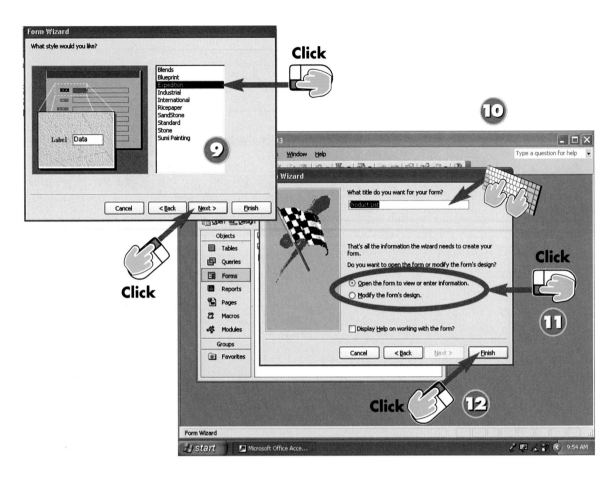

The wizard presents a list of styles that affect how the form looks (such as its colors, background, fonts, and so on). Click a style to preview it. When you find one you like, click **Next**.

10 Type a name for the form in the **What title do you want for your form?** field; the form will be saved with this name.

11 Select whether you want to open the form immediately (shown here) or modify the form's design first.

12 Click **Finish**.

Saving the Form

TIP

When you use the Form Wizard to create a form, that form is saved automatically using the name you type for that form in step 10. You do need to save the form manually, however, if you make any changes to the form's design later.

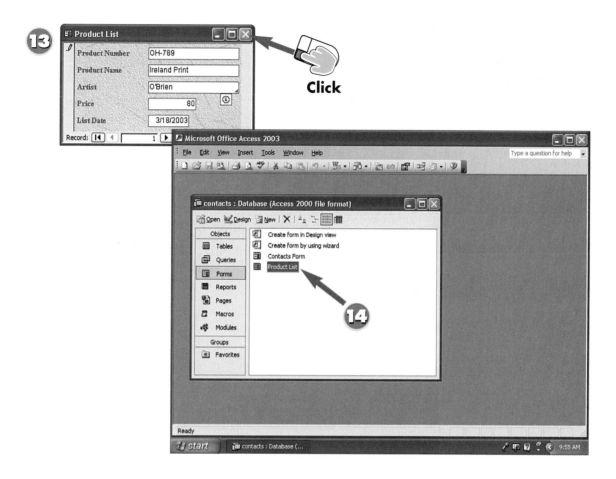

Depending on your selection in step 11, Access displays the new form in Datasheet view (for viewing and entering records) or Design view (for changing the form's design). Click its **Close** button.

The form is listed in the database window; you can open the form again when you want to use it.

AutoForm Versus Wizard
The wizard offers the same layout choices as the AutoForm but provides additional choices on which fields you can include, as well as different styles.

Including Multiple Tables
For more complex forms, you can include fields from more than one table. You can also base a form on a query (queries are covered in Part 6). For more information, see Access's Help system.

Saving a Form

Start

Click

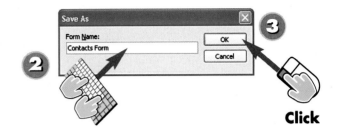

Click

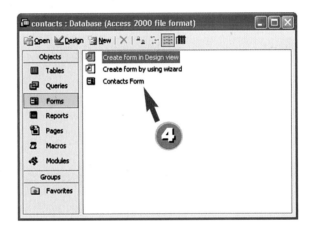

1 Open the **File** menu and choose **Save**. If you are simply saving changes to an existing form's design, the form will be saved.

2 If you are saving a new form for the first time, Access prompts you to type a name for the form. Do so in the **Form Name** field.

3 Click **OK**.

4 The form is saved. When you close the form, you'll see it listed in the database window with the name you typed in step 2.

End

When you create an AutoForm or a form from scratch, you need to save the form, assigning it a name. The name you assign is how the form will be listed in the database window. You also need to save a form if you make changes to the form's design.

TIP
Clicking the Save Button
If you prefer, you can click the **Save** button in the toolbar to save the form.

TIP
Closing a New Form Without Saving
If you close a new or edited form without saving it first, you are prompted to save it. Click **Yes** to save the form.

Opening a Form

Start

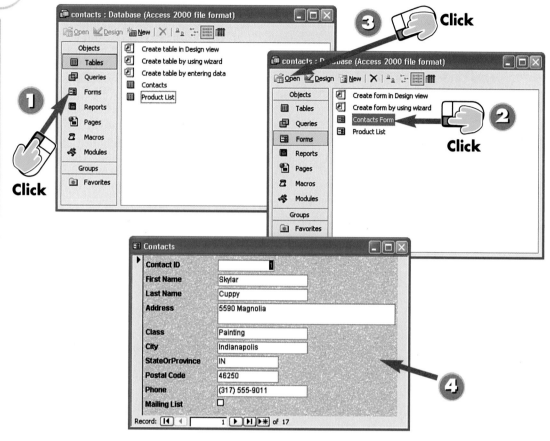

Click **Click** **Click**

1. After you open the database that contains the form you want to use, click the **Forms** option in the Objects bar.

2. Forms you have created for this database are listed. Click to select the form you want to open.

3. Click the **Open** button in the database window's toolbar.

4. The selected form is displayed.

End

When you want to enter or view records using a form, you need to open the form first. You do so from the database window.

TIP

Opening and Closing Forms
If you prefer, you can double-click the form in the database window to open it. To close a form, click its **Close** button.

Using a Form to Add a New Record

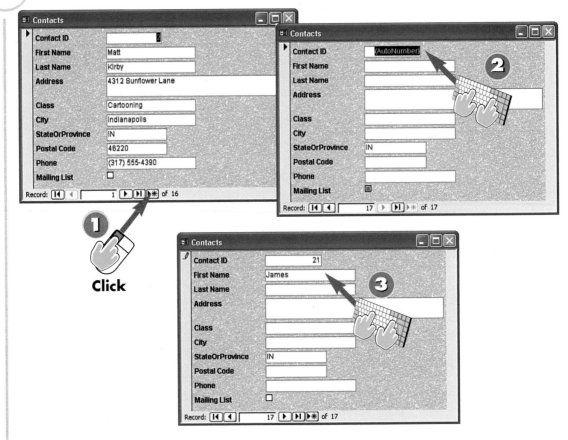

Click

---

1 After you've opened the form you want to use to add a new record, click the form's **New Record** button.

2 The form changes to contain a blank record with the first field selected. In this case, the first field is an AutoNumber field, so press the **Tab** key on your keyboard to move to the next field.

3 The insertion point moves to the next field (here, the First Name field). Type an entry (in this case, **James**) and press the **Tab** key.

One of the main purposes of a form is to enter new records. To create a new record, you simply display a blank record and then complete the fields.

AutoNumber Fields
Some tables include *an AutoNumber field*, whose value is automatically entered and incremented. That is, you do not type an entry into this field; Access does it for you. Press **Tab** to move to the next field.

Using the Toolbar
If you prefer, you can click the **New Record** button in the Standard toolbar found in the main Access window to begin entering a new record.

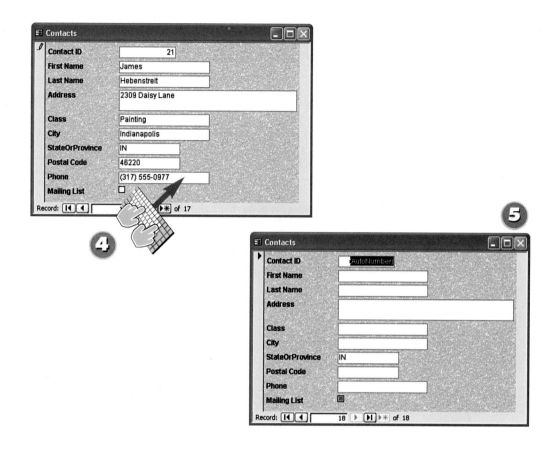

4 Continue typing entries and pressing the **Tab** key until the record is complete.

5 When you press **Tab** after completing the last field, Access saves the record and displays a new blank one, ready for your entries.

End

Viewing All Records
When you click the New Record button in a column/row form layout, Access hides all existing records so that you can focus on just the record you are working on. To redisplay all records, open the **Records** menu and choose **Remove Filter/Sort**.

Modifying a Form
After you've used a form a few times, you may notice ways in which the form could be improved. Fortunately, Access enables you to change the form's design. This part includes several tasks on modifying the form's design.

Default Entries
If you set up any default entries for the table on which your form is based, those fields in the form will already be complete, for example, here "IN" for the StateOrProvince field. You can always override the entry by typing a new one.

Using a Form to Display Records

Start

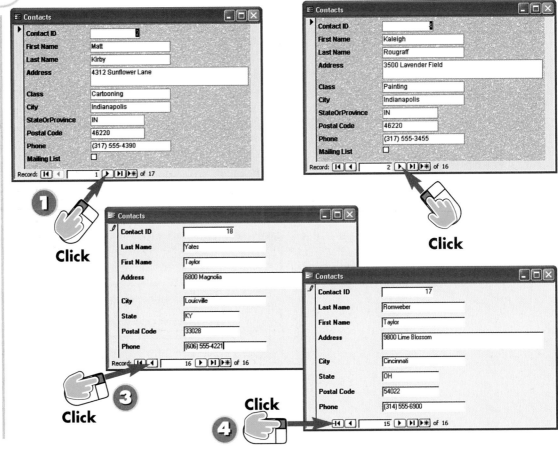

Click

Click

Click

Click

End

1. After you've opened the form associated with the table whose records you want to display, click the form's **Next** button to display the next record.

2. You see the next record (notice that the navigation bar lists the record number as well as the total number of records). Click the **Last Record** button to display the last record in the table.

3. The last record (in this case, record 16) in the table is displayed. Click the **Previous** button to display the previous record (that is, record 15).

4. The second-to-last record (record 15) is displayed. Click the **First Record** button display the first record in the table.

You can use the navigation buttons in a form to move from record to record. You can move to the next or previous record, or to the first or last record.

TIP

Adding a New Record
The navigation bar also includes a button for creating a new record. You can click this button or the button in the Standard toolbar in the main Access window to create a new record. For more information, refer to the task "Using a Form to Add a New Record" earlier in this part.

Using a Form to Edit Data

Start

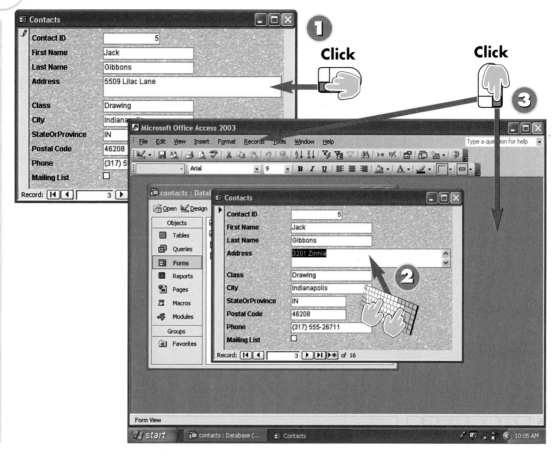

Click

Click

1 After you've displayed the record you want to modify, click in the field you want to change.

2 Delete the entry and type a new one, or edit the existing entry.

3 Click anywhere outside the field to save the changes. Alternatively, open the **Records** menu and choose **Save Record**.

End

In addition to entering data into a table using a form, you can also use a form to make changes to the data, just as you do in Datasheet view. Your changes to a field are saved when you move the insertion point out of that field.

Selecting an Entry
When you press Tab to move to a field, the entire entry is selected. You can start typing to replace the existing entry with a new entry.

TIP

Using a Form to Select Records

Start

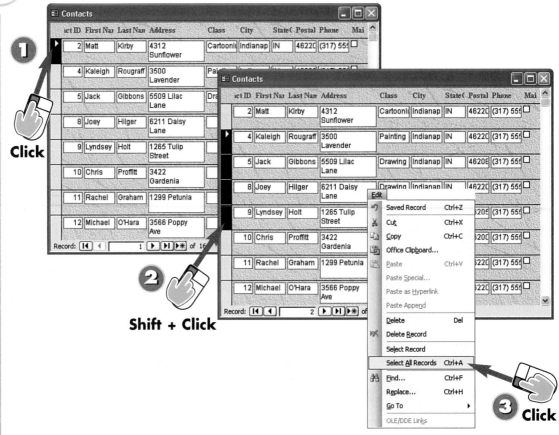

Click

Shift + Click

Click

1. To select a single record, click the table cell where the record selector column (farthest to the left) and the record row intersect. An arrow appears next to the selected record.

2. To select a series of records, click to select the first record, press and hold down the **Shift** key, and click the last record. The first and last records, and all records in between, are selected.

3. To select all records, open the **Edit** menu and choose **Select All Records**.

End

When you want to work with a single record (perhaps to delete that record) or a set of records, you start by selecting the record. In a form that displays one record at a time, you can display that record and then make any changes. If the form uses a layout similar to a datasheet, however, you can select a single record, a set of records that are next to each other, or all records. (You can select multiple records only in the datasheet-type form.)

TIP

Using the Select All Shortcut

If you prefer, you can press **Ctrl+A** to select all records.

Using a Form to Delete a Record

Start

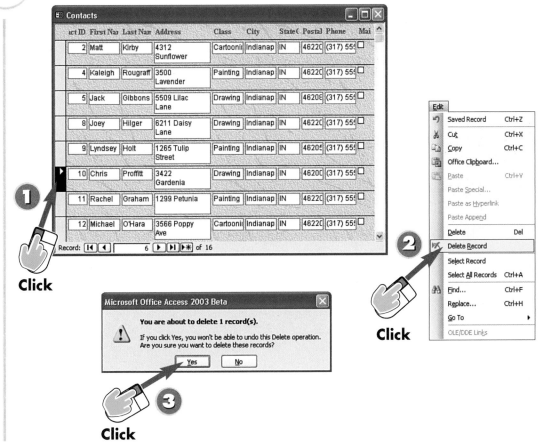

Click

Click

Click

① Select the record you want to delete.

② Open the **Edit** menu and choose **Delete Record**.

③ Access prompts to confirm the deletion; click **Yes**. The record is deleted.

End

INTRODUCTION

No doubt there will be a time when you want to delete records that you no longer need. For example, you might delete records that are no longer pertinent or are outdated. One way to delete records is to use a form.

Caution
You cannot undo a record deletion, so be sure that you really do want to delete the record. Access prompts you to confirm the deletion.

Using the Delete Record Button
If you prefer, you can click the **Delete Record** button on the Standard toolbar in the main Access window. Or you can press the **Delete** key to delete a record.

Using a Form to Search for a Record

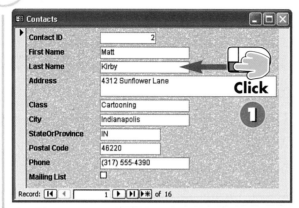

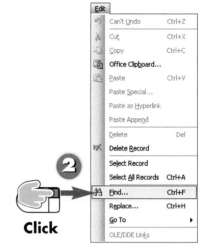

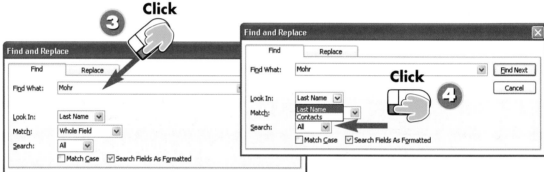

1 With any record in the form displayed onscreen, click in the field on which you want to search (in this example, the **Last Name** field).

2 Open the **Edit** menu and choose **Find**.

3 The Find and Replace dialog box opens. Type the entry you want to find (here, **Mohr**).

4 The field selected in step 1 is displayed in the **Look in** text box. To instead search the entire form, click the **down arrow** next to the text box and choose the form's name in the list that appears.

INTRODUCTION

Just like you can search for a record in a datasheet, you can also search in a form. Doing so can help you quickly locate a certain record or set of records. You might search to display a record for editing, or to review a record before making a sales call. You can search on any of the fields in the form.

TIP

Using the Find Button and Shortcut Key
If you prefer, you can click the **Find** button on the Standard toolbar in the main Access window rather than use the Edit menu to open the Find and Replace dialog box. Alternatively, you can press the Find shortcut (**Ctrl+F**) key on your keyboard.

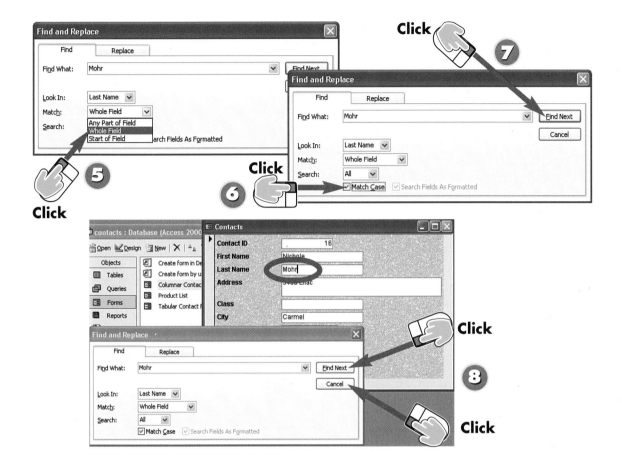

Click

Click

Click

Click

Click

Click

5 Click the down arrow next to the **Match** field and select to view matches to the whole field, any part of the field, or the start of the field.

6 To match the case as you've entered it, check the **Match Case** check box.

7 Click **Find Next**.

8 Access displays the first matching record, with the matching entry highlighted. To view the next matching record, click **Find Next**; when you're finished searching, click **Cancel**.

End

Moving the Dialog Box
You may need to move the Find and Replace dialog box to view the matches. Click and drag the dialog box's title bar to move the dialog box out of the way.

Continuing the Search
If the first match isn't the one you want, you can click the **Find Next** button in the Find and Replace dialog box until you find the record you need.

No Matches Found?
Access displays an alert message to notify you if no matches are found. If that happens, try changing the search options; perhaps the search is too limiting. Alternatively, try searching on a different field, or on the entire table.

Filtering Data by Selection

Start

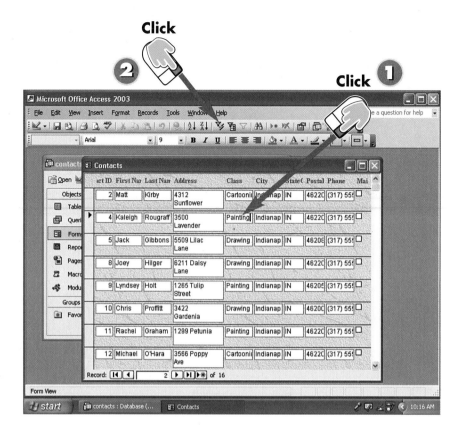

1. After you open the form that you want to use to filter data, click in an instance of the entry you want to use as the filter (here, a **Painting** entry in the Class field).

2. Click the **Filter By Selection** button on the Standard toolbar in the main Access window.

There may be times when you want to focus on a particular set of records. For example, you might want to display all records in a certain state, all records of a certain product type, or, as outlined here, all records of people who are taking a particular class. The easiest way to display a set of records is to use Access's Filter by Selection feature. You'll view the results as a whole in a datasheet form, but you can also filter data using single-form views. Only those that match the filter will be available for scrolling.

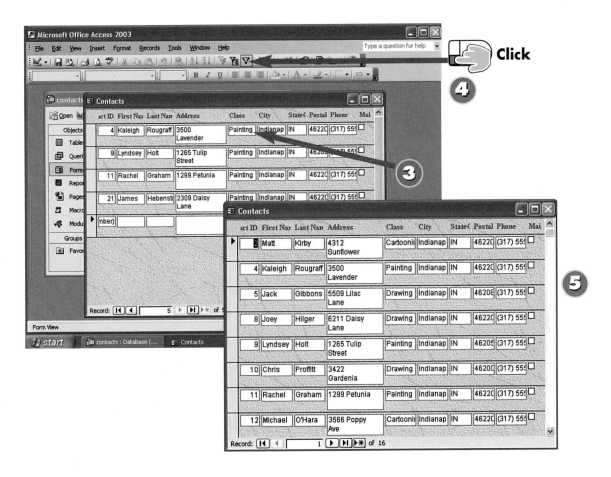

Click

Access displays only those records that contain that entry in the selected field (in this example, those records that contain a **Painting** entry in the Class field).

To again view all records in the table, click the **Remove Filter** button on the Standard toolbar in the main Access window.

All records are displayed again.

End

Using the Menus

If you prefer, you can open the **Record** menu, choose **Filter**, and choose **Filter By Selection** instead of clicking the Filter By Selection button in step 2.

Filtering by Exclusion

In some cases, you may want to display all records that *don't* contain a specific entry. In that case, you can filter excluding the selection by opening the **Records** menu, choosing **Filter**, and selecting **Filter Excluding Selection**.

Filtering Again

You can further filter the subset of records by filtering on another field. For example, in a customer form, you might filter for all records in South Carolina and then filter the records to display those assigned to a particular sales representative.

Filtering Data by Form

Start

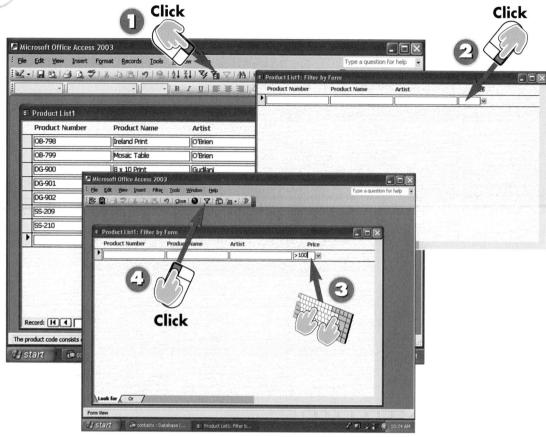

1. After you open the form that you want to use to filter data, click the **Filter By Form** button on the Standard toolbar in the main Access window.

2. A blank record containing all the fields in the form appears. Click in the field that you want to filter by.

3. Type the entry you want to match, or type a filter expression. For example, to find all products over $100, type **>100** in the **Price** field.

4. Click the **Apply Filter** button on the Standard toolbar in the main Access window.

If you don't want to simply search for an entry, you can use your form to create a filter. This method enables you to enter criteria in a blank form to select a range of records that match that criteria. For example, suppose that you want to display all products that cost $100; you can type **100** in the blank Price field to locate all records that meet that criterion. If, on the other hand, you want to find all products that cost *more* than $100, you could do so by creating a filter expression. *Filter expressions* use mathematical operators such as less than (<), greater than (>), equal to (=), and so on to select a range of records.

Click

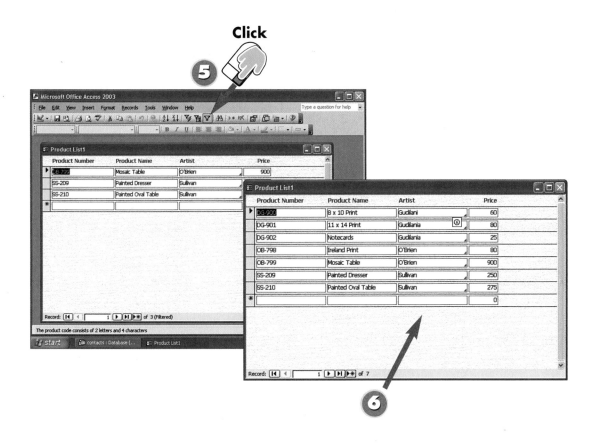

5 Access displays all the records that match the criteria you entered. To again view all records in the table, click the **Remove Filter** button on the Standard toolbar in the main Access window.

6 All records are again displayed.

End

Toggling the Apply/ Remove Filter Button
The Apply/Remove Filter button is a *toggle*. That is, when the data is not filtered, the Apply Filter button is present. When the data is filtered, the button changes to the Remove Filter button.

Creating Complex Filter Expressions
You can create complex filter expressions using other types of operators. For even more instruction, consult Access's online help.

Using the Drop-Down List
If you prefer, you can click the down arrow next to the selected field and choose an entry instead of typing the entry in step 3. This is the same as creating a Filter By Selection.

Viewing a Form in Design View

Start

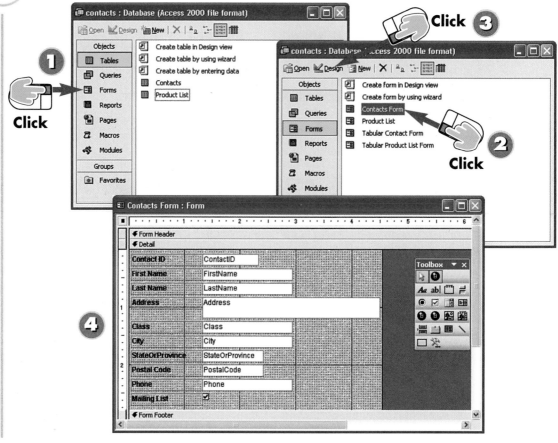

Click 1

Click 3

Click 2

4

1. After you open the database that contains the form you want to view in Design view, click the **Forms** option in the Objects bar.

2. Click the form you want to modify or view.

3. Click the **Design** button in the database window's toolbar.

4. The form opens in Design view and is divided into three sections: Form Header, Detail, and Form Footer. You can add items to or remove items from each of these sections.

When you create a form using a wizard or an AutoForm, you may find that you need to make some changes to it to better suit your needs. To do so, you view the form in Design view, which shows you the underlying structure of the form. Likewise, if you want to create a form from scratch, you'd do so in this view. This task shows you how to view a form in Design view; you'll learn how to modify a form in later tasks.

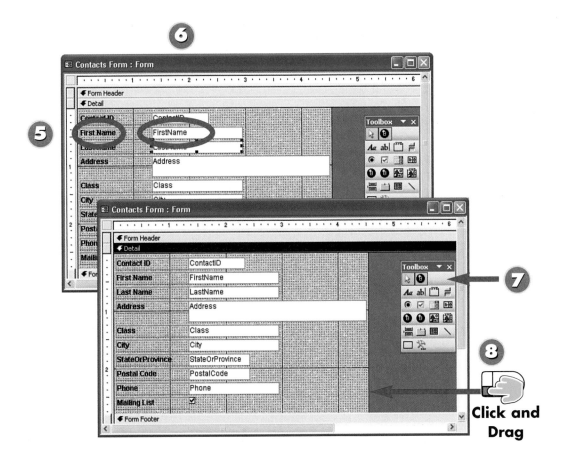

Click and Drag

5️⃣ The form is created through the use of *controls*. Some controls are labels and display the name of the field.

6️⃣ Other controls, called *text box controls*, pull data from the table to display in the form.

7️⃣ Note the Control toolbox. This palette of buttons lets you add, select, and modify the controls on the form.

8️⃣ All the controls are placed on the form. You can resize the entire form if needed by dragging its border.

End

Using the Ruler
Design view includes a ruler to help you place and align items on the form.

Toolbox not Displayed?
If the toolbox is not displayed, open the **View** menu and choose **Toolbox**. (You can close the toolbox by clicking its **Close** button.)

Creating a Form from Scratch
If you want to create a form from scratch, you could select to create a blank form by selecting **Create form** in Design view from the database window. Then display the field list and add the fields you want to include.

Selecting a Form Control

Start

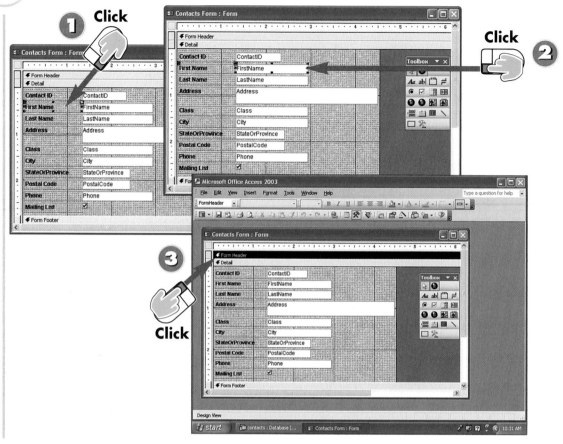

Click ①

Click ②

③

Click

① To select a label control, click it. Only the label is selected. Notice the move and resizing handles that appear around the edge of the label.

② To select a text box control, click it. When you select a text box, both the text box and its associated label are selected.

③ To select a form section (Form Header, Detail, or Form Footer), click the section divider. The section is selected.

End

INTRODUCTION

As mentioned, a form consists of elements called controls. Certain controls are labels, such as the labels for a field name; these are, by default, bound to the text box control that displays data from that field (also called the *data field*) . When you want to move, resize, or delete a control, whether it's a label control or a text box control, you start by selecting it.

TIP

Selecting Multiple Controls
To select more than one control, click the first control, and then press and hold down the **Ctrl** key as you click on each additional control you want to select.

Deleting a Field from a Form

Start

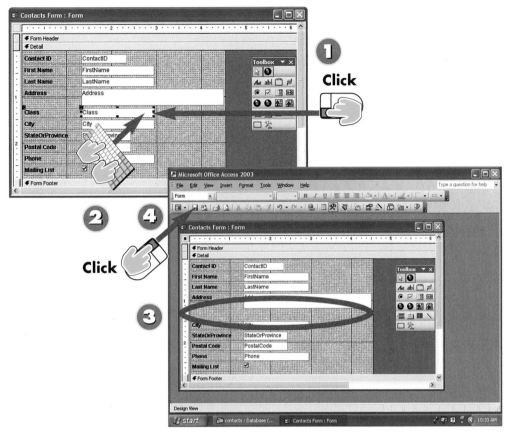

Click

2 **4**

Click

3

1 After you open the form that contains the field you want to delete in Design view, click the field's text box control to select both the label *and* the text box.

2 Press the **Delete** key on your keyboard.

3 The field is deleted.

4 Click the **Save** button on the Standard toolbar in the main Access window to save the change to the form.

End

INTRODUCTION

If you decide that you no longer need a field that appears on your form, you can easily delete it.

TIP

Undoing the Deletion
If you change your mind, you can undo the deletion by clicking the **Undo** button on the Standard toolbar in the main Access window or by opening the **Edit** menu and choosing **Undo**.

Resizing a Form Control

Start

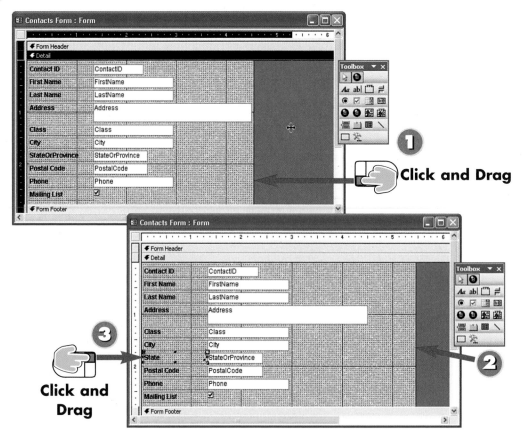

Click and Drag

Click and Drag

1. To change the size of the form, put the pointer on the form border and drag.

2. The form is resized.

3. To resize a label, click it to select it, and then drag one of the sizing handles (any black box except for the bigger box in the upper-left corner) until the label is the size you want.

If the contents of a field name or field entry are not completely displayed in a form (a common occurrence when you use a row and column–style layout), you can resize the control, be it the field's label control, text box control, or both. In addition, you can resize the entire form as needed to make room.

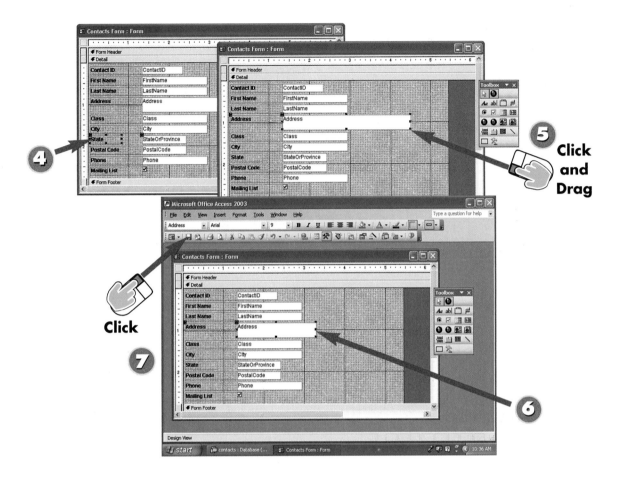

**Click
and
Drag**

Click

4 The label is resized (here, made smaller).

5 To resize a text field, click it to select it, and then drag any of the sizing handles (except for the bigger box in the upper-left corner) until the text field is the size you want.

6 The text field control is resized (again, made smaller).

7 Click the **Save** button on the Standard toolbar in the main Access window to save the change to the form.

End

No Automatic Adjustments

Access does not make an automatic adjustment if one control overlaps another. You need to manually move and resize the controls so that they don't overlap.

Moving a Form Control

Start

Click and Drag

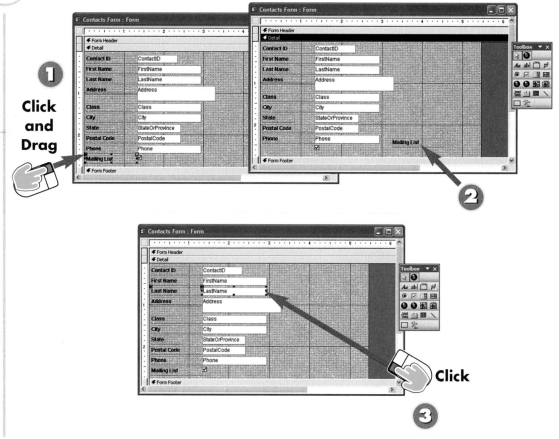

Click

1. To move a label, click it to select it, and drag the selection handle (the larger black box) in the upper-left corner.

2. The label is moved.

3. To move both the label and the text field, click the text field to select both controls.

INTRODUCTION

One change you may want to make to your form is to rearrange the order of the fields it contains. For example, in a columnar table, you might want to balance the fields better by moving one field to another column. Or, you might want to move a label away from its text box to provide more space between the two. You can move a label, the text box, or both the label *and* the text box.

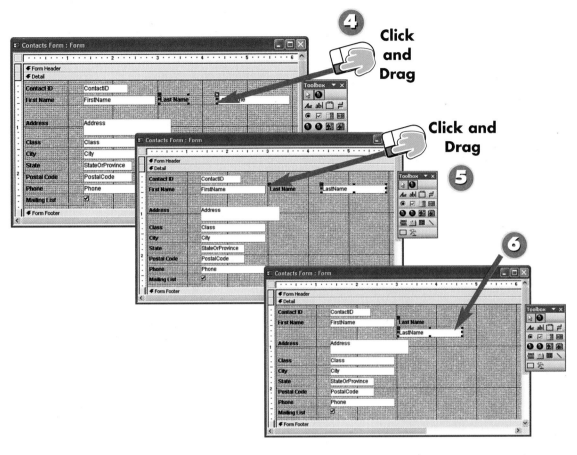

Click and Drag

Click and Drag

4️⃣ Click within the label (not on the selection box), and drag the fields to a new location. Notice that both the label and the text box are moved.

5️⃣ To move just the text field, select it, and then drag the selection handle in the upper-left corner of the text field (not the label).

6️⃣ Just the text field is moved. Click the **Save** button on the Standard toolbar in the main Access window to save the changes to the form design.

End

Changing the Tab Order
Note that changing the field order does not change how you move through the fields when you press the Tab key during data entry. To make this change, you must change the Tab order. To learn how, see the task "Changing the Tab Order" later in this part.

TIP

Adding a Field to a Form

Start

Click ①

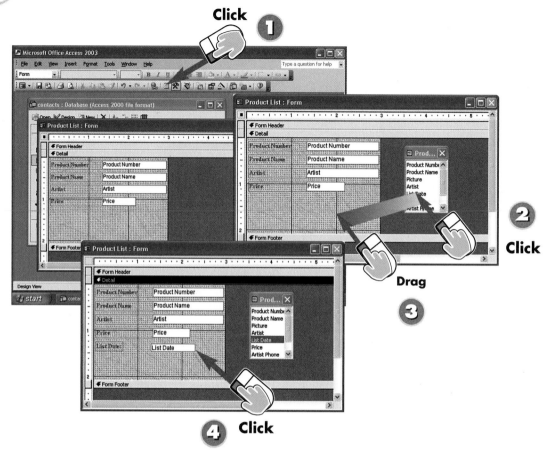

Click ②

Drag ③

Click ④

1. After you open the form to which you want to add a field in Design view, click the **Field List** button on the Standard toolbar in the main Access window.

2. A list of fields in the current table appears. Click the field you want to add to select it.

3. Drag the field to the location on the form where you want it to be placed.

4. Access adds a label and text box for the new field. (You may have to make some adjustments to the field's size and placement.) Click the **Save** button to save the form design.

End

When you create a form with a wizard, you select which fields are included. If needed, however, you can add more fields to the form later. You can even add fields from other tables.

Resizing Sections
You may need to resize the Detail section of the form to make room for the new field. To do so, place the mouse pointer on the section's border and drag it to resize.

Using Menu Commands
If you prefer, you can open the **View** menu and choose the **Field List** command to display the list of fields in the current table. To close the list, click its **Close** button.

Changing the Tab Order

Start

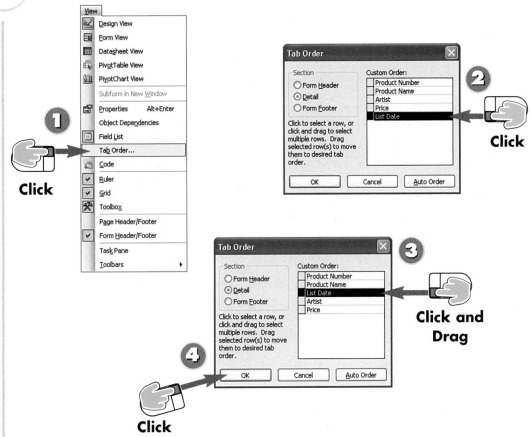

Click

Click

Click and Drag

Click

1. After you've opened the form whose Tab order you want to change in Design view, open the **View** menu and choose **Tab Order** to open the Tab Order dialog box.

2. The Tab Order dialog box displays the form's Tab order. Click a field whose place in the Tab order you want to change to select it.

3. Click the selected field and drag it to its new spot in the order.

4. Repeat steps 2 and 3 until the fields are arranged in the order you want. When you're finished, click **OK**.

End

INTRODUCTION

When you press the Tab key on your keyboard while entering data into a form, Access moves the insertion point to the next field in the database table. You might, however, prefer to enter information in a different order. In that case, you can change the form's Tab order. When you change a form's Tab order, you won't notice a change to the form's layout, but you will notice a change when you use the form to enter data.

TIP

Selecting Multiple Fields?
If you keep selecting multiple fields instead of dragging the field, it's because you haven't released the mouse button after clicking. Remember to click once to select, release the mouse button, and then click and drag the field to the new location.

Viewing and Formatting Form Controls

Start

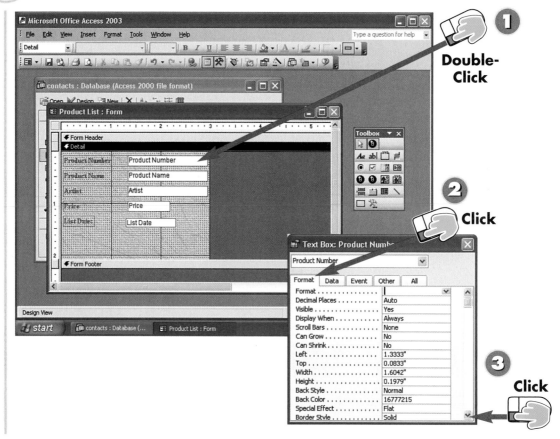

Double-Click

Click

Click

① After you've opened the desired form in Design view, double-click the form control you want to modify.

② A control-specific dialog box opens. Click the **Format** tab if it is not selected already.

③ The Format tab contains the various formatting options. Click the scroll arrows to scroll through the list.

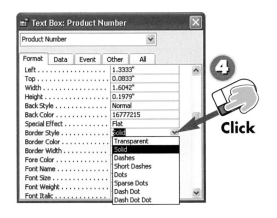

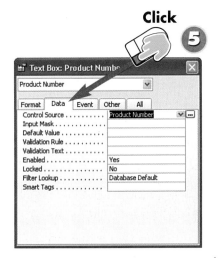

4 Click in a text field. In some cases, such as with the Border Style option, a down arrow appears on the right side of the field; click it to display a list of formatting options.

5 Click the dialog box's **Data** tab to view the various Data options. (Some of these options are the same as the field properties for a field in a table.)

6 Click the **Other** tab to view additional options that you can change, such as the field name.

End

Formatting Forms

Start

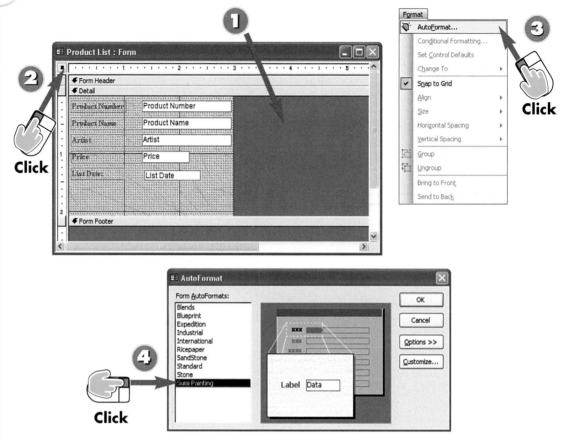

Click

Click

Click

1. Open the form you want to format in Design view, and make sure that none of the form elements are selected.

2. Select the entire form by clicking the blank box in the upper left corner at the top of the form.

3. Open the **Format** menu and choose **AutoFormat**.

4. The AutoFormat dialog box appears, displaying a list of available formats. Click a format to preview it. When you find a format that you want to use, click **OK**.

Click

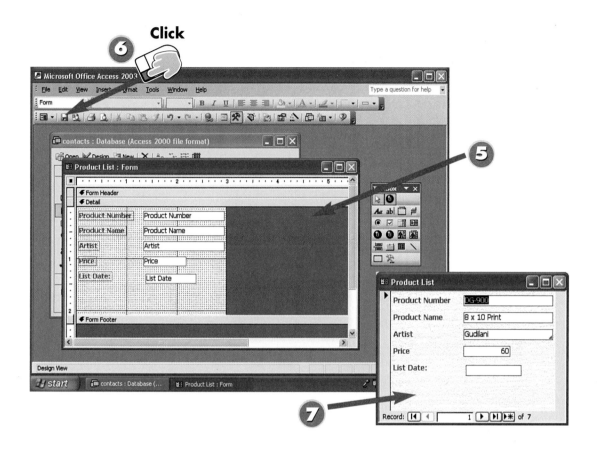

5️⃣ Access applies the selected AutoFormat to the form.

6️⃣ Click the **Save** button on the Standard toolbar in the main Access window to save the change to the form.

7️⃣ To see how the new form will look when you enter data, close the form and then reopen it.

End

Selecting AutoFormat Options

To specify which aspects of the AutoFormat are applied, click the **Options** button in the AutoFormat dialog box. Then uncheck any of the options you don't want to use (font, color, or border) .

More Form Options

For a complete list of options, similar to those for formatting a control, double-click the box to the left of the ruler to select the entire form. Doing so displays the properties for the form. You can then review and make any changes, similar to those for modifying a control. You can also apply settings to sections of a form; double-click the section and then make changes as needed to the section properties.

Creating Queries

Often, you don't want to work with all the data in a database; just a subset or group of specific records. For instance, you might want to view all your customers in South Carolina. Or you might want to view all products with a low inventory. For this purpose, Access enables you to create a query. Using a query, you can instruct Access to select and display a set of records from a table that match the criteria you enter.

You base a simple query on a single table, and that query pulls data from the table. You can also build more sophisticated queries that pull data from multiple tables. (This topic is not covered in this book.)

The simplest way to get started building a query is using a wizard, but you can also build a query from scratch. This part covers both methods, as well as how to save, run, and modify a query.

field list ➤

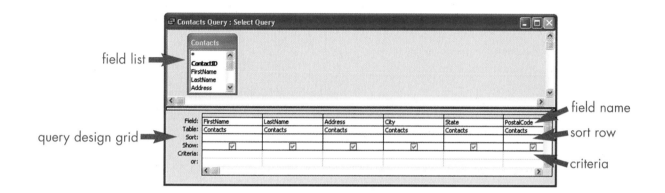

query design grid ➤

field name

sort row

criteria

Creating a Select Query with a Wizard

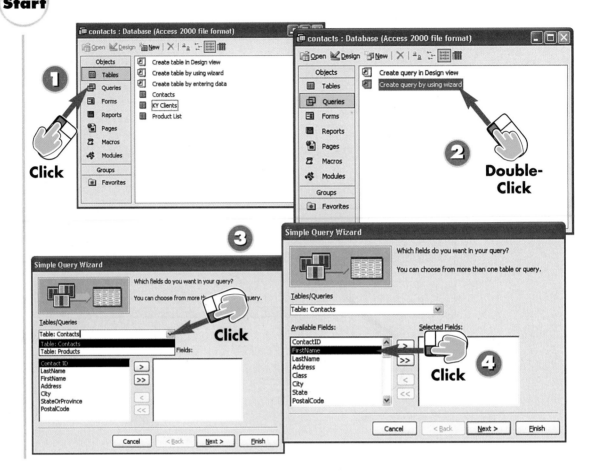

Start

Click

Double-Click

Click

Click

1. After you've opened the database on which you want to base a query, click the **Queries** button in the Objects bar.

2. Double-click the **Create query by using wizard** option.

3. The Simple Query Wizard starts. Click the **down arrow** next to the **Tables/Queries** field and choose the table on which you want to base the query from the list that appears.

4. The **Available Fields** list includes all the fields in the selected table. Click the first field that you want to include in the query (here, **FirstName**) .

INTRODUCTION

Unlike other wizards, the Simple Query Wizard creates a table of sorts, which you use to select the fields you want to include in the query. The wizard then creates a simple select query, where you can type the value to match in Query Design view. A *select query* selects records that match the value you enter. (To create a different type of query, simply enter the necessary criteria to the query you build here; you'll learn how later in this part.)

TIP

Selecting a Table
Pick the table that contains that data you want to search and pull specific entries from. For instance, if you want to create a query with product inventory results, use the product inventory table.

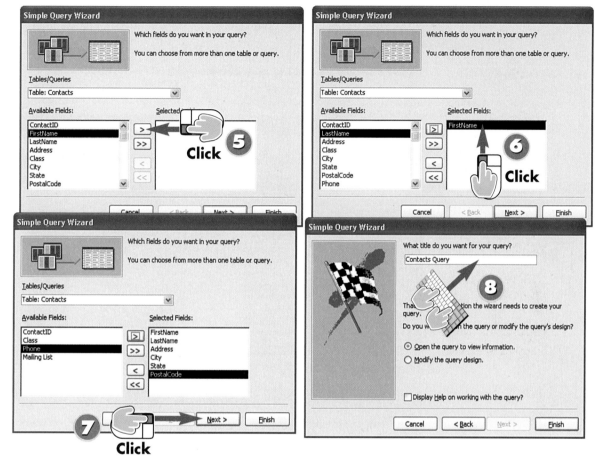

5. Click the **Add** button (the one that contains a single right-pointing arrow).

6. The field is added to the **Selected Fields** list. Continue selecting and adding fields until all the fields you want are added.

7. When all the desired fields have been added, click the **Next** button.

8. The next screen of the Simple Query Wizard opens. In the **What title do you want for your query** field, type a name for the query; the query will be saved with this name.

See next page

Adding and Removing Fields

If you want to include in your query all the available fields in a table, skip steps 4 and 5 and instead click the **>>** button in the first screen of the Select Query Wizard. To remove a field from the **Selected Fields** list, click the field to select it, and then click the **<** button.

Creating a Select Query with a Wizard (Continued)

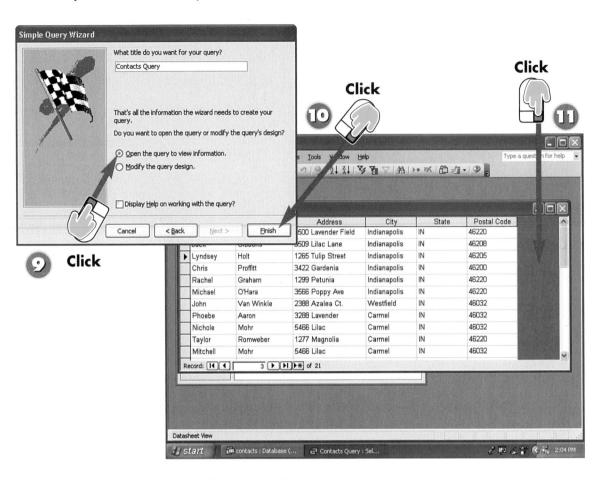

⑨ To open the query, click the **Open the query to view information** option button, as shown here. (Alternatively, to make changes to the query, choose **Modify the query design**.)

⑩ Click the **Finish** button.

⑪ Access displays the select query you have created, which consists of a table that contains the fields you selected. You next need to build the criteria as covered later in this part.

End

Building a Query from Scratch

Start

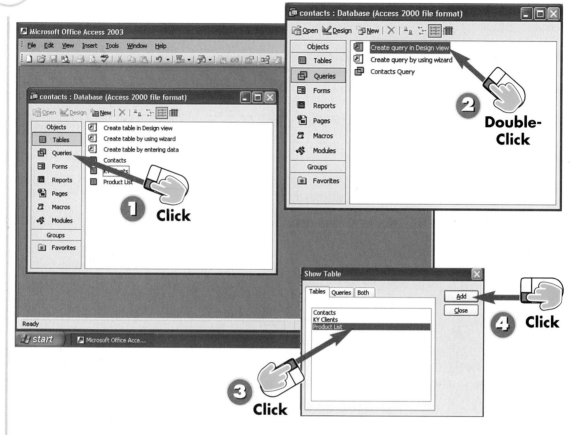

1 After you've opened the database on which you want to base a query, click the **Queries** button in the Objects bar.

2 Double-click the **Create query in Design view** option.

3 The Show Table dialog box opens, displaying a list of the tables contained in the open database. Click the table you want to use for your query.

4 Click the **Add** button to add a list of the fields in the selected table to the Design window.

See next page

INTRODUCTION

In addition to using a wizard to select the fields for a query, you can also build a query from scratch using the Design view to add the fields. As with the wizard, you still need to enter the criteria for the query after you build it from scratch; you'll learn how later in this part.

TIP

Pulling from Multiple Tables
If you want, you can create a query that pulls data from multiple tables; simply select the tables from the Show Table dialog box. For information on building a query with fields from multiple tables, consult Access's online help.

Building a Query from Scratch (Continued)

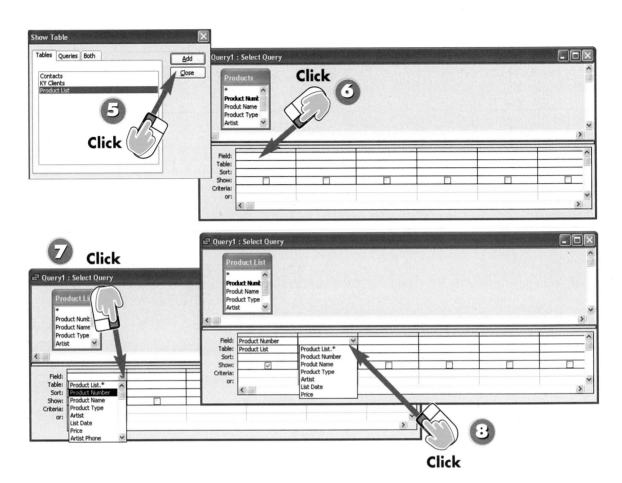

5. Click the **Close** button in the Show Table dialog box to close it.

6. Click in the **Field** box in the lower half of the Query Design window; a down arrow appears.

7. Click the **down arrow** in the **Field** box and choose the first field that you want to add to the query from the list that appears.

8. The field is added. To add another field, click the box immediately to the right of the field you just added. A down arrow appears; click it and choose the field you want to add.

Dragging Fields

TIP

If you prefer, you can drag a field from the field list to the **Field** column in the design grid.

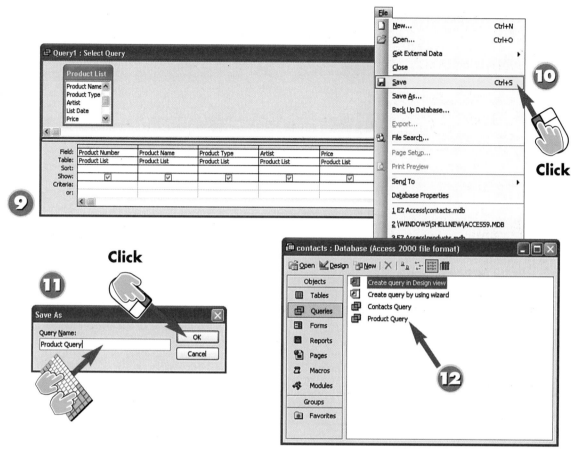

Click

Click

9. Continue adding fields until the query contains all the fields you need.

10. You now have the structure for your query and are ready to save and name it. To begin, open the **File** menu and choose **Save**.

11. The Save As dialog box opens. Type a name for the query in the **Query Name** field and click **OK**.

12. The query is saved. When you close the query, it will be listed in the database window under the name you typed in step 10.

Saving the Query

TIP

If you prefer, you can click the **Save** button on the toolbar to open the Save As dialog box. If you try to close the query without saving first, you will be prompted to save; click **Yes** to save the query.

Viewing the Query Design

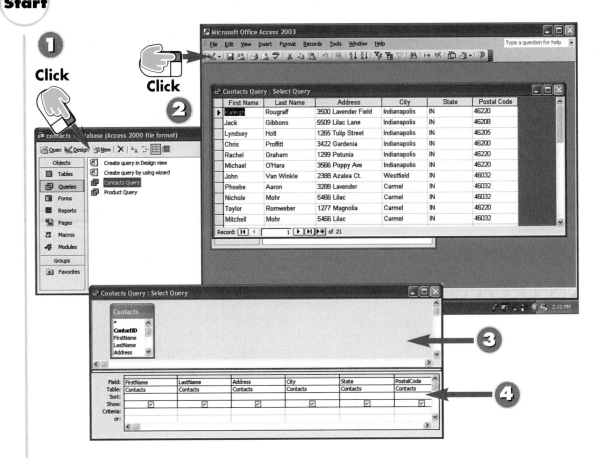

1 If the query is not already open, select it in the database window and then click the **Design** button in the toolbar in the database window.

2 If the query is open, click the **Design** button in the main Access window's Standard toolbar.

3 The query design window opens. The top part of the design window contains the list of fields in the table on which the query is based.

4 The bottom part of the design window contains a grid that displays each of the fields you selected when you created the query as well as the table in which each field resides.

Switching to Design View
If you are using a wizard to build a query, the query will be open, and you can simply switch to Design view. If you are modifying an existing query, you'll start from the database window, click the **Queries** option in the Objects bar, select the query you want to open, and then click the **Design** button.

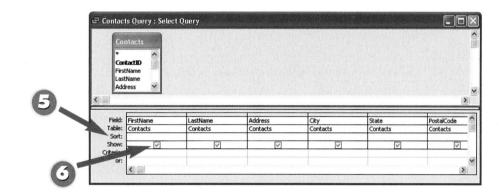

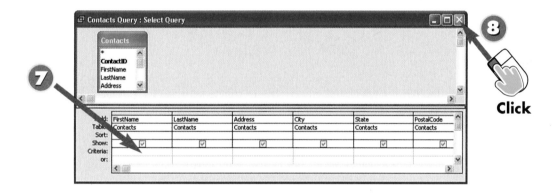

Click

5 Use the Sort row to specify which field is used to sort the query. (See the task "Sorting Query Results" later in this part for more information.)

6 If you do not want to display a field in the query results but still use that field for building criteria, uncheck it.

7 Use the Criteria row to enter the value or range you want to match. Other tasks in this part provide several examples of entering criteria.

8 To close the query design window, click its **Close** button.

End

Entering Criteria to Query for an Exact Match

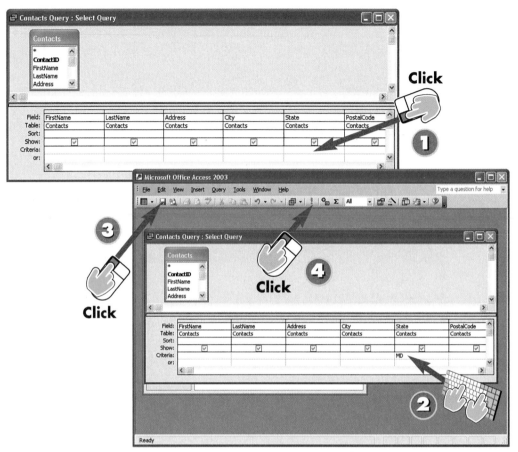

Start

Click ①

Click ③

Click ④

②

1. After you've displayed the query for which you want to enter criteria in Design view, click in the cell in the **Criteria** row for the field you want to match.

2. Type the value you want to match. In this instance, type **MD** in the **State** field to find all clients who live in the state of Maryland. Access automatically adds quotation marks around your entry.

3. Click the **Save** button on the Standard toolbar in the main Access window to save the query design.

4. Click the **Run** button to run the query.

INTRODUCTION

Suppose that you want to find all clients who live in a particular state. In that case, you'd query for an exact match—that is, you'd enter criteria to enable your query to pull all records that match a particular entry in a particular field (in this example, all entries in the State field that contain the value **MD**).

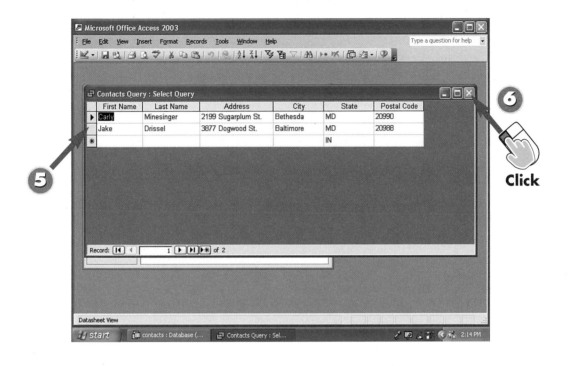

Click

5. Access runs the query and displays a table containing only those records that match the criteria you entered (in this case, clients in Maryland) .

6. Click the **Close** button to close the query.

End

Blank Record?
If you have set up a default value for entering data, you will see a blank record as part of the results. This may be confusing, but it's how Access works.

Running the Query Again
You can run (or *open*) the query again at any time. To learn how, see the task "Running a Query" later in this part.

Modifying the Query
You can modify the query—change the criteria to match or add other criteria[md]as needed. See the other tasks in this part to learn how.

Entering Criteria to Query for a Range of Matches

Start

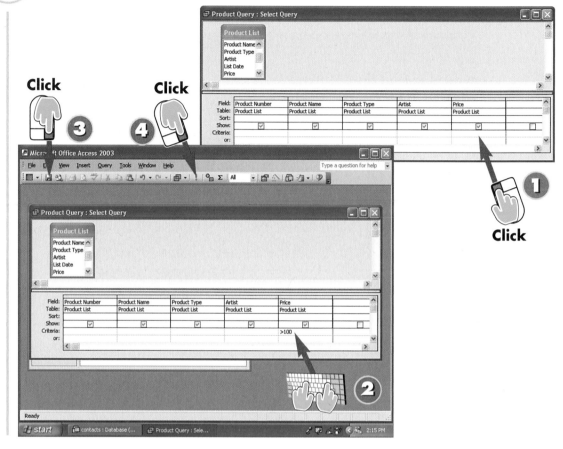

Click ③

Click ④

Click ①

Click ②

After you've displayed the query for which you want to enter criteria in Design view, click in the cell in the **Criteria** row under the field you want to use as the comparison (here, **Price**).

Type the criteria expression. For example, to find all products priced at more than $100, type **>100** under the **Price** field.

Click the **Save** button on the Standard toolbar in the main Access window to save the query design.

Click the **Run** button to run the query.

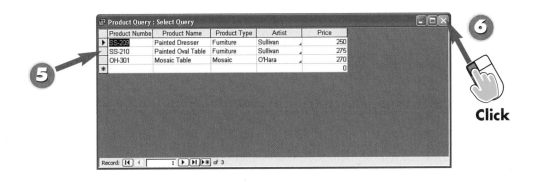

Click

5 Access runs the query and displays a table containing only those records that match the criteria you entered (in this case, products priced more than $100).

6 Click the **Close** button to close the query window.

End

Using Expressions
TIP
For more information on using expressions in your queries, consult Access's online help.

Entering Multiple Criteria with the OR Operator

Start

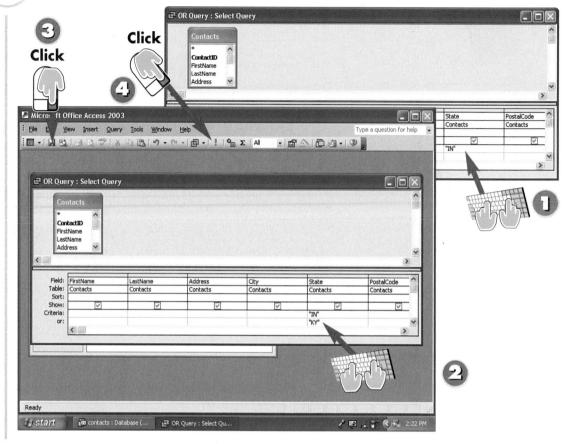

① After you've displayed the query for which you want to enter criteria in Design view, click the cell in the **Criteria** row for the field you want to match, and type your first criterion (here, **IN**).

② Click in the **or** row in the same column, and type the second value you want to match (in this case, **KY**).

③ Click the **Save** button on the Standard toolbar in the main Access window to save the query design.

④ Click the **Run** button to run the query.

INTRODUCTION

There may be times when you want to match more than one criteria. For instance, you might want to list all clients who live in Indiana, as well as those clients who live in Kentucky, as outlined here. To do so, you use the **OR** operator.

TIP

Quotation Marks
Access will automatically add quotation marks around your entry. You'll see these if you move to another field or open the query.

	First Name	Last Name	Address	City	State	Postal Code
	Chris	Proffitt	3422 Gardenia	Indianapolis	IN	46200
	Rachel	Graham	1299 Petunia	Indianapolis	IN	46220
	Michael	O'Hara	3566 Poppy Ave	Indianapolis	IN	46220
	John	Van Winkle	2388 Azalea Ct.	Westfield	IN	46032
	Phoebe	Aaron	3288 Lavender	Carmel	IN	46032
	Nichole	Mohr	5466 Lilac	Carmel	IN	46032
	Taylor	Romweber	1277 Magnolia	Carmel	IN	46220
	Mitchell	Mohr	5466 Lilac	Carmel	IN	46032
	Andrew	Hilger	6211 Daisy Lane	Indianapolis	IN	46220
	Taylor	Yates	3244 Petunia St.	Louisville	KY	50441
	Rae	Sigmon	4988 Sweat Pea	Louisville	KY	50433

OR Query : Select Query

Record: 1 of 14

Click

5 Access runs the query and displays a table containing only those records that match the criteria you entered (in this case, clients in Indiana or Kentucky).

6 Click the **Close** button to close the query window.

End

Entering Criteria to Match More Than One Field

Start

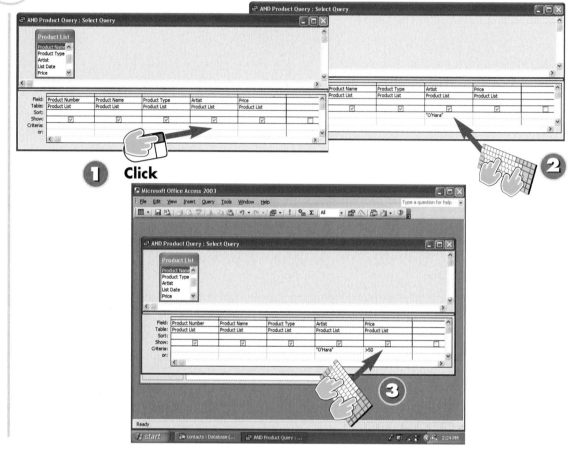

1 Click

1 After you've displayed the query for which you want to enter criteria in Design view, click the cell in the **Criteria** row for the first field you want to match (here, **Artist**).

2 Type the first criterion (in this example, **O'Hara**).

3 Click in the second field you want to match (here, **Price**) and type your second criterion—in this example, **>50** (to find all pieces by the artist that cost more than $50) .

INTRODUCTION

In addition to running a query to match one or more values in a single field, you can also create a query that requires a match in more than one field. For example, you might run a query to return a list of products by a particular artist within a certain price range, as shown here.

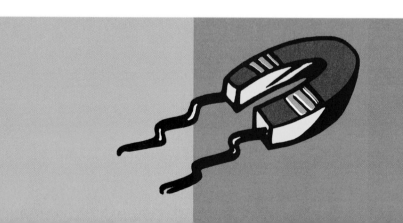

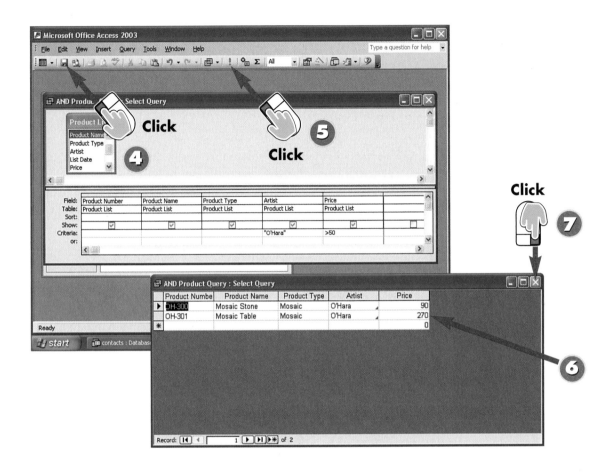

Click the **Save** button on the Standard toolbar in the main Access window to save the query design.

Click the **Run** button to run the query.

Access runs the query and displays a table containing only those records that match the criteria you entered (here, all products by artist O'Hara with a price more than $50).

Click the **Close** button to close the query window.

End

AND Queries
This type of query is sometimes called an *AND query* because the data in the selected table must match both the first criteria *and* the second criteria to be included in the results.

Criteria
For the criteria, you can type a value to match or build an expression using operators (>, <, =, and so on) .

Sorting Query Results

Start

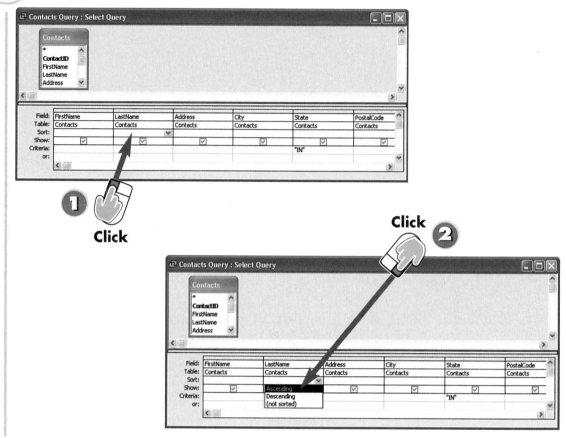

Click

Click

After you've entered your criteria, click in the **Sort** row under the field by which you want to sort. For example, to sort results by last name, click in the **Sort** row under the **Last Name** field.

A down arrow appears. Click the **down arrow** and choose **Ascending** or **Descending** from the list that appears.

INTRODUCTION

In addition to selecting a set of records, you can optionally sort the records in a query using the Sort row. That way, you can view the results in the order you select. You can sort in ascending or descending order.

Click ③ **Click** ④

Click ⑥

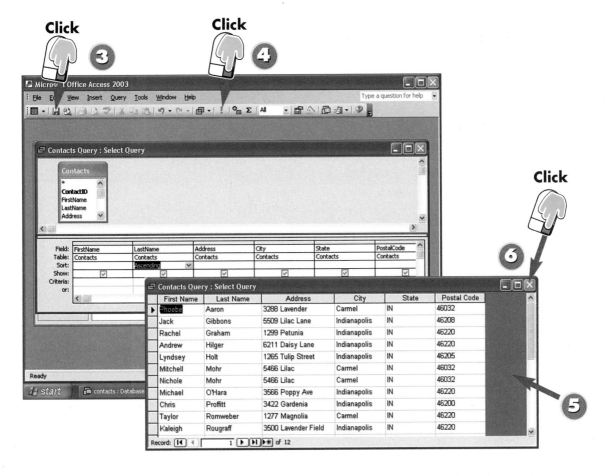

③ The sort order is entered. Click the **Save** button on the Standard toolbar in the main Access window to save the change you made to the query.

④ Click the **Run** button to run the query.

⑤ Access runs the query and displays the results, sorted in the order you selected (in this case, all clients in Indiana, sorted by last name).

⑥ Click the **Close** button to close the query.

End

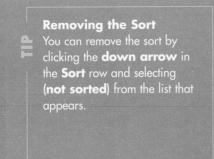

Removing the Sort
You can remove the sort by clicking the **down arrow** in the **Sort** row and selecting (**not sorted**) from the list that appears.

Starting Over
To clear the existing criteria and sort options, open the **Edit** menu and choose **Clear Grid**.

Adding a Field to a Query

Start

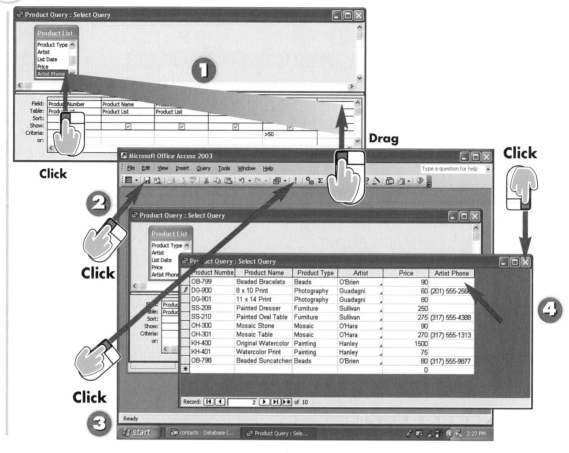

Click

Drag

Click

Click

Click

Click

① After you've displayed the query you want to modify in Design view, click the field you want to add in the field list and drag it to an empty column.

② The field is added. Click the **Save** button on the Standard toolbar in the main Access window to save the query design.

③ Click the **Run** button to run the query.

④ Access runs the query and displays the results; the field you added (in this case, **Artist Phone**) is included. Click the **Close** button to close the query.

INTRODUCTION

Suppose that you forgot to add a particular field when you built your query. If so, you can use the list of fields that appears in the query design window to add fields to the query.

Change Field Order

TIP

You can also change the order in which the fields are listed in the query. To do so, click right above the field name. Then drag the column to the location you want.

Removing a Field from a Query

Start

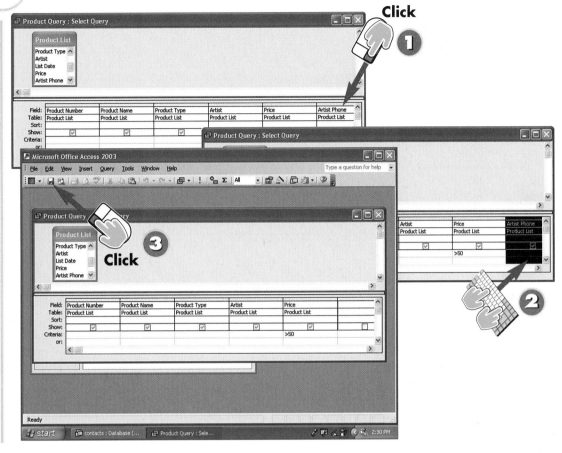

Click

1

① After you've displayed the query you want to modify in Design view, click above the field you want to delete.

② The column is selected. Press the **Delete** key on your keyboard.

③ The field is removed. Click the **Save** button on the Standard toolbar in the main Access window to save the query design. When you run the revised query, this field will not be included.

End

If you included fields in your query that are not pertinent to the query results, you can delete the fields. For example, if you used a wizard to build your query, you might have started with all the fields in the table and then realized that you only needed a select few. If so, you can remove any fields you don't need.

Hiding Fields

TIP

If you prefer, you can simply *hide* a field. For example, suppose that you need to use a field in your criteria, but you don't necessarily have to display that field in your results. To hide it, uncheck the check box under the field's name in the **Show** row.

Saving a Query

Start

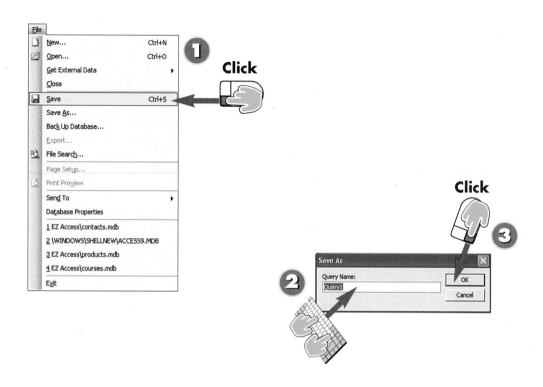

Click

Click

1 Open the **File** menu and choose **Save**. If you are saving changes to an existing query, the Save process is complete; if you are saving a query for the first time, proceed to step 2.

2 The Save As dialog box opens. Type a name for the query in the **Query Name** field.

3 Click **OK**. The query is saved. When you close the query, it will be listed in the database window with the name you typed in step 2.

End

INTRODUCTION

When you create a query using a wizard, it is saved automatically with the name you specify. If you create a query from scratch, however, you'll need to name and save it manually. In addition, you must save a query after making changes to the query's design, such as adding criteria, or adding or removing fields.

TIP

Saving the Query
If you prefer, you can click the **Save** button on the toolbar to open the Save As dialog box. If you try to close the query without saving first, you will be prompted to save; click **Yes** to save the query.

Running a Query

Start

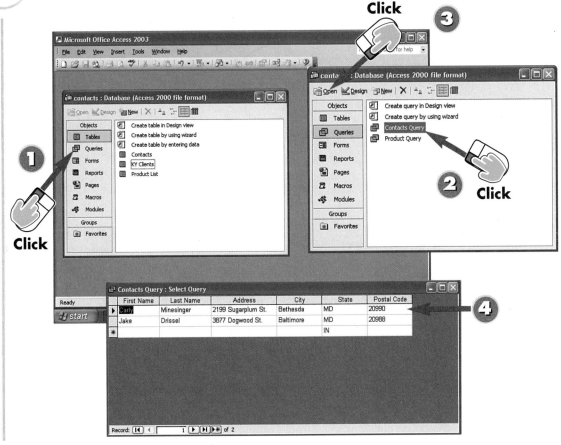

1. After you've opened the database that contains the query, click the **Queries** option in the Objects bar.

2. Any queries you have created and saved are listed. Click the query you want to open.

3. Click the **Open** button in the database window's toolbar.

4. Access runs the query and displays the results.

End

INTRODUCTION

When you want to view the results of a query, you run or open the query from the database window.

Opening and Closing Queries

If you prefer, you can double-click a query in the database window to open it. To close a query, click its **Close** button.

Editing and Adding Data

If you change or add data to a query, the associated database table is updated to reflect those changes. In this way, you can use a query to edit and add data.

Creating a New Table with Query Results

Start

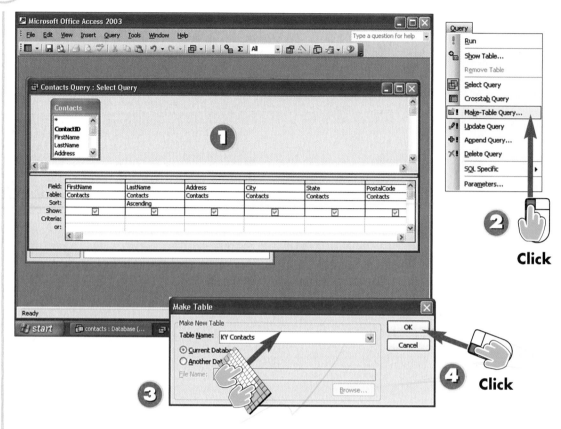

Click

Click

1. Create a query that includes the fields you want to use in the new table, and set up the query's criteria to select the records you want placed in the new table.

2. Open the **Query** menu and choose **Make-Table Query**.

3. The Make Table dialog box appears. Type a name for the new table in the **Table Name** field.

4. Click **OK**.

INTRODUCTION

One way to use queries is to pull certain records from a database table and use those records to create a new table. For example, suppose that you want to create a new database table of clients from a certain state. You can do so by creating a make-table query.

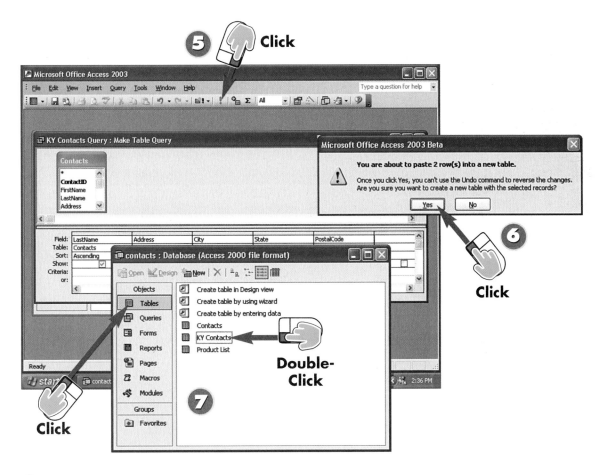

5 Click **Click** the **Run** button on the Standard toolbar in the main Access window.

6 Access displays a message explaining that a new table will be created with the records contained in the query results. Click **Yes** to create the table.

7 The new table is listed in the database window with the name you specified. (To view the table, close the query, click **Tables** in the database window's Objects bar, and double-click the table name.)

New Table

Because the make-table query replaces the original query on which it is based, it's a good idea to create a new query for this action. Alternatively, save the make-table query with a different name (see the next tip).

Using the Save As Command

When you modify a query's design, the new query (in this case, the make-table query) replaces the query you started with. If you want to keep the original query, save the new query under a new name by opening the **File** menu, choosing **Save As,** and typing a new query name in the dialog box that appears.

Deleting Records with a Query

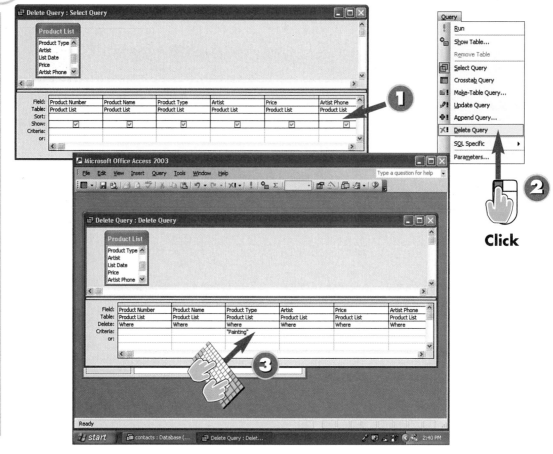

① Build a new query that contains the fields you want to search, but with no criteria entered.

② Open the **Query** menu and choose **Delete Query**.

③ The design grid changes to include a Delete row. Set the query's criteria to return the records you want to delete (here, all records containing a **Painting** entry in the **Product Type** field) .

INTRODUCTION

Suppose that you want to delete a certain product type from your inventory. Rather than deleting each instance of that product type in your database, you can use a delete query to both select the records to be deleted and then delete them.

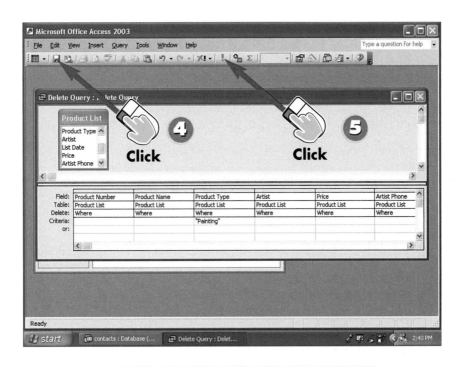

Click the **Save** button on the Standard toolbar in the main Access window to save the query.

Click the **Run** button.

Access displays a message explaining that records will be deleted from the table. Click **Yes** to delete the records.

No Undo

You cannot undo this action, so be sure that the query you create will return the correct records and that you do, in fact, want to delete those records. If not, click **No** when prompted to confirm the deletion.

Other Query Types

You can also create queries to update records in a table. For example, you might use a query to update the price of a product instead of manually changing each record. You can also create a query to append (add) records to a database table. This is useful if you are working with multiple tables.

Creating Reports

There will almost certainly be times when you want to create a summary of data in your Access database in a printed format, called a report. For example, you might include a report in a sales presentation, or as part of your company's annual report. Alternatively, you might create a report to generate a simple list of clients and their phone numbers. Access provides many features for creating reports, from simple reports that list data, to complex reports that can sort, perform calculations, and group data.

Access also provides several methods for creating a report: creating an AutoReport, using a wizard, and building one from scratch. This part covers how to create a report using an AutoReport and wizard, how to make changes to the report's design, and how to preview and print the report.

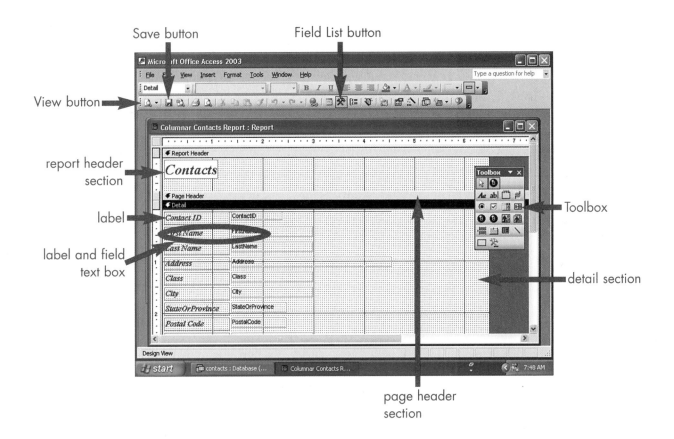

Save button

Field List button

View button

report header section

label

label and field text box

Toolbox

detail section

page header section

Creating an AutoReport

Start

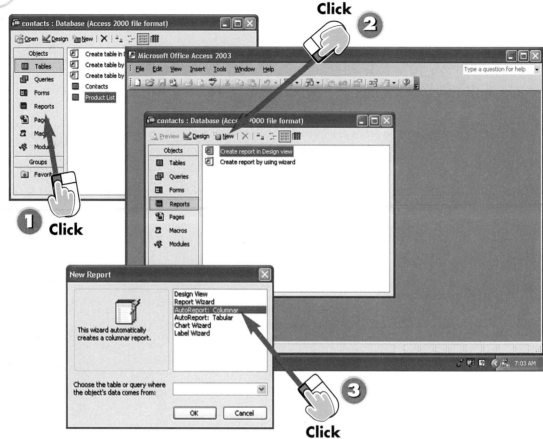

Click **2**

1 Click

3 Click

1 After you've opened the database for which you want to create a report, click the **Reports** option in the database window's Objects bar.

2 Click the **New** button in the database window's toolbar.

3 The New Report dialog box opens. Depending on the type of report you want to create, click either **AutoReport: Columnar** or **AutoReport: Tabular** to select it.

Access has several *AutoReports* that are excellent tools for quickly creating simple reports with columnar or tabular layouts. (You can also use AutoReports to create labels and charts, but these options are not covered in this book.) AutoReports include all the fields from the table on which the AutoReport is based.

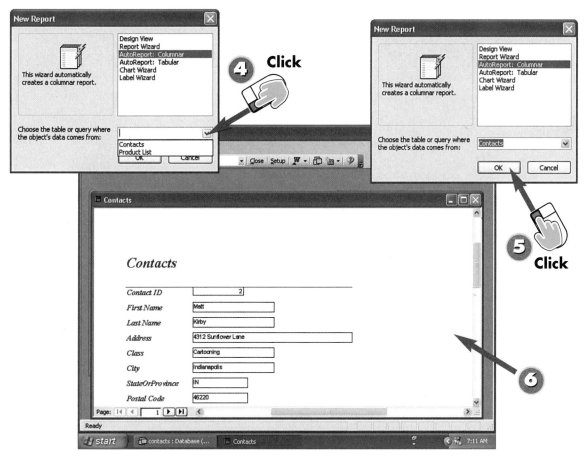

4 Click the **down arrow** next to the **Choose the table or query...** field and choose the table on which you want to base the report.

5 Click **OK**.

6 Access creates a report (here, a columnar report from a contact database) and displays the report's first page.

End

Saving a Report
When you create a new report, you must save and name it, just as you do when you create a new table, form, or query. See the task "Saving a Report" for more information.

Scrolling Through Report Pages
Most reports include more than one page. To view additional pages in the report, use the page buttons at the bottom of the page to scroll to the next, previous, first, and last pages in the report. You can also preview the report in a special preview window; see the task "Previewing a Report" later in this part for more information.

Creating a Report Using a Wizard

Start

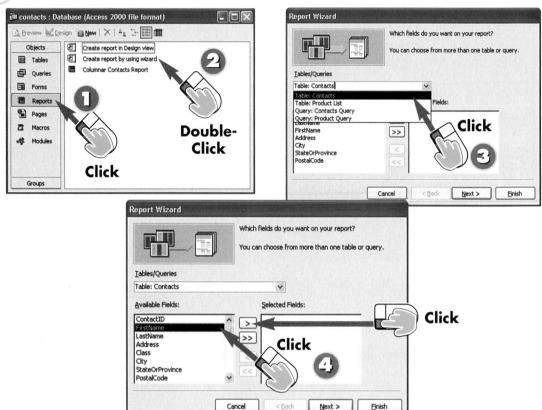

① After you've opened the database for which you want to create a report, if necessary, click the **Reports** option in the database window's **Objects** bar.

② Double-click the **Create report by using wizard** option to start the Report Wizard.

③ The Report Wizard starts. Click the **down arrow** next to the **Tables/Queries** field and choose the table on which you want to base the report from the list that appears.

④ The **Available Fields** list includes all fields in the selected table. Click the first field that you want to include in the report (here, **FirstName**), and then click the **Add (>)** button.

Using Access's AutoReport feature is great if all you want to do is create a simple columnar or tabular report that contains information from all the fields in the selected table. If, however, you want your report to use a more varied layout, or to include only certain fields in the selected table, you can use the Report Wizard to create a report.

Adding and Removing Fields

If you want to include in your report all the available fields in a table, click the **>>** button for step 4. To remove a field, click the field to select it and then click the **<** button.

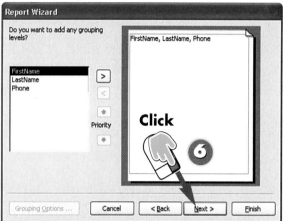

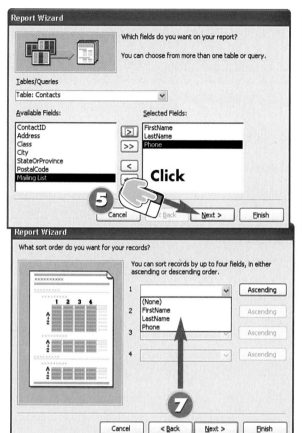

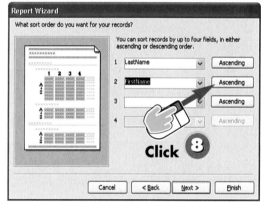

5 The field is added to the **Selected Fields** list. Continue selecting and adding fields until all the fields you want appear and then click the **Next** button.

6 Optionally, add grouping levels for the report. (See the tip on this page for more information about grouping levels.) When finished, click **Next**.

7 Access asks you how the fields in the report should be sorted. Display the first drop-down list and choose the first sort field; repeat for any additional fields you want to use to sort.

8 The default sort order for each field is ascending. To sort a field in descending order, click the **Ascending** button next to that field; the button changes to read "Descending."

See
next
page

Grouping a Report

You can group a report into sections. For example, you might group a product report by type so that all types are listed under the product type heading. To find out more about grouping items in a report, see the task "Sorting and Grouping Data in a Report" later in this part. _P 196_

Sorting on More Than One Field

If you want to sort on more than one item, first select the first sort field and order. Then, click in the second sort box, and select the next sort field and order. Using the wizard, you can sort by as many as four fields.

Creating a Report Using a Wizard (Continued)

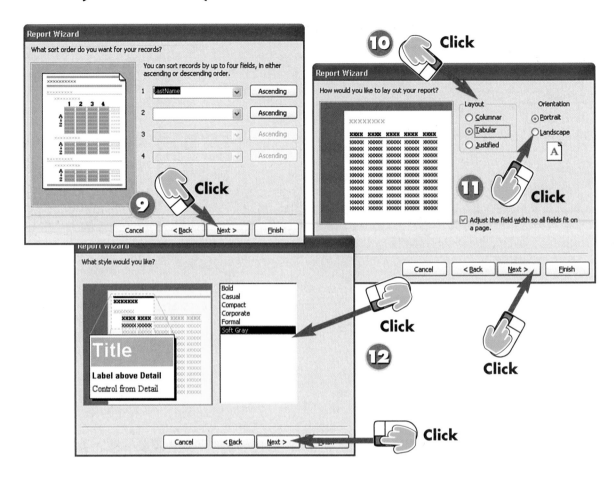

9 Repeat step 8 for any other fields you want to sort in descending order. After you finish making your sort-order selections, click the **Next** button.

10 In the **Layout** area, click the **Columnar**, **Tabular**, or **Justified** option button; a preview of the selected layout appears.

11 In the **Orientation** area, click **Portrait** if the report does not contain many fields; if the report contains several fields, click **Landscape** to fit more across the page. Then click **Next**.

12 Click one of the options in the list to select a style for your report; preview the selected style on the left. When you find a style you like, click **Next**.

Layout Choices

In a tabular report, all records are listed in rows across the page. A columnar report is similar to a form, where you see one record at a time; all the record information is listed in a rectangular area. Unlike a form, each record is listed one after another in the report. The justified layout is similar to the columnar report only the record data is spread out margin to margin and different formatting (dark borders) are used to separate records.

Fitting Data on One Page

If you want Access to adjust the field width to fit all the selected fields on one page, click the **Adjust the field width so that all fields fit on a page** check box before clicking **Next** in step 12.

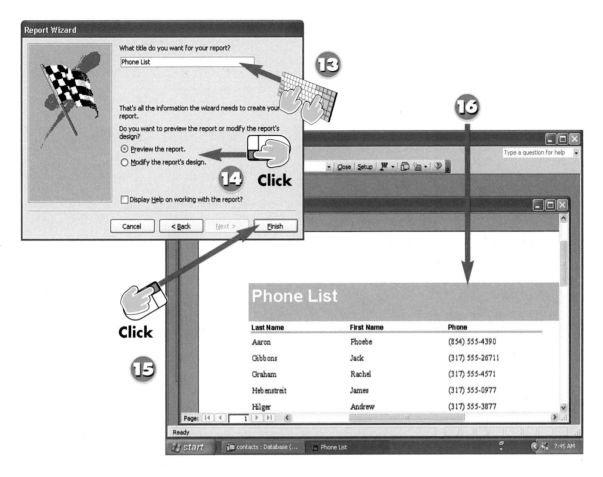

13 The next screen of the Report Wizard opens. In the **What title do you want for your report** field, type a name for the report; the report will be saved with this name.

14 To preview the report, click the **Preview the report** option button, as shown here. (Alternatively, to make changes to the report, choose **Modify the report's design**.)

15 Click the **Finish** button.

16 Access displays the report you created (here, a simple phone list).

End

Saving the Report
When you use a wizard to create a report, that report is saved automatically using the name you typed in step 13. If you make changes to the report's design later, however, you need to resave the report. For help, see the task "Saving a Report" later in this part.

Saving a Report

Start

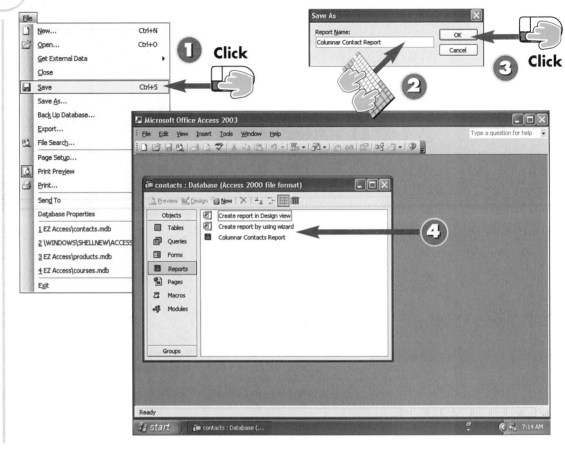

Click ①

Click ③

②

④

① Open the **File** menu and choose **Save**. If you are saving changes to an existing report, the Save process is complete; if you are saving a report for the first time, proceed to step 2.

② The Save As dialog box opens. Type a name for the report in the **Report Name** field.

③ Click **OK**.

④ The report is saved. When you close the report, it will be listed in the database window with the name you typed in step 2.

End

When you create a report using the Report Wizard, it is saved automatically with the name you specify. If you create an AutoReport or a report from scratch (not covered in this book), however, you'll need to name and save it manually. In addition, you must save a report after making changes to the report's design.

Using the Save As Command

When you modify a report's design, the new version of the report replaces the report you started with. If you want to keep the original report, save the new report under a new name by using the **File**, **Save As** command. Type a new name.

Saving the Report

If you prefer, you can click the **Save** button to save a report. If you try to close a report without saving first, you will be prompted to save; click **Yes** to save the report.

Opening a Report

Start

1 Click

2 Double-Click

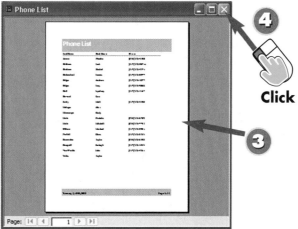

4 Click

3

1. After you've opened the database that contains the report you want to open, click the **Reports** option in the Objects bar (if that option is not selected already).

2. Any reports you have created and saved are listed. Double-click the report you want to open.

3. Access opens the report.

4. To close the report, click the **Close** button.

End

INTRODUCTION

Before you can view or print a report, you must open it. You do so from the database window.

Viewing a Report's Design

Start

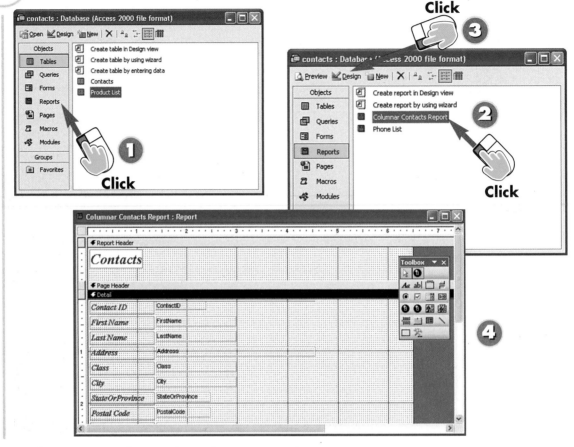

1 After you open the database that contains the report you want to view in Design view, click the **Reports** option in the Objects bar (if that option is not selected already).

2 Click the report you want to modify or view.

3 Click the **Design** button in the database window's toolbar.

4 The report opens in Design view and is divided into several sections: Report Header, Page Header, Detail Area, Page Footer, and Report Footer. You can add items to each of these sections.

When you create a report using the Report Wizard or AutoReport, you may find that you need to make some changes to it to better suit your needs. To do so, you view the report Design view, which shows you the underlying structure of the report. Likewise, if you wanted to create a report from scratch, you'd do so in this view. This task shows you how to view a report in Design view; you'll learn how to modify a report in later tasks.

Using the Ruler
The Design view includes a ruler to help you align items on the report.

TIP

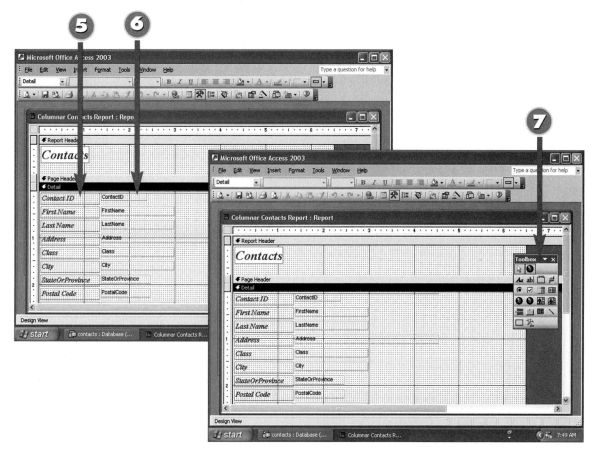

5 The report is created through the use of *controls*. Some controls are *labels* and display the name of the field; these are usually bound to the control that contains the data for that field.

6 Other controls, called *text box controls*, pull data from the table to display in the report.

7 Note the Control toolbox. This palette of buttons lets you add, modify, and select the items on the report.

Working with Controls
See the next tasks for more information on working with controls.

Toolbox Not Displayed?
If the Control toolbox is not displayed, open the **View** menu and choose **Toolbox**. You can close the toolbox by clicking its **Close** button.

Report Header/Footer Versus Page Headers/Footers
The *report* header and footer appear only on the first page of the report. The *page* headers and footers appear on all pages in the report except the first, although you can change these defaults.

Selecting a Report Control

Start

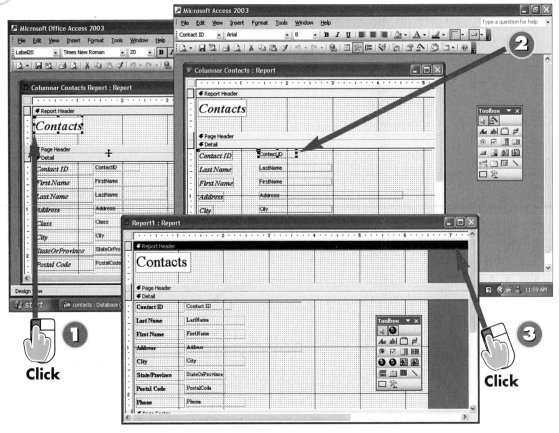

Click

Click

1. To select a label control, click it. Only the label is selected. Notice that a *move handle* and *sizing handles* appear around the edge of the label.

2. To select a text box control, click it. When you select a text box, both the text box and its associated label are selected.

3. To select a report section (Report Header, Page Header, and so on), click the section divider.

End

INTRODUCTION

As mentioned, a report consists of elements called *controls*. Certain controls are labels, such as the labels for a field name; these are, by default, bound to the text box control that displays data from that field (also called the data field). When you want to move, resize, or delete a control, whether it's a label control or a text box control, you start by selecting it.

TIP

Selecting Multiple Controls
To select more than one control, click the first control, and then press and hold down the **Ctrl** key as you click on each additional control you want to select.

Deleting a Field from a Report

Start

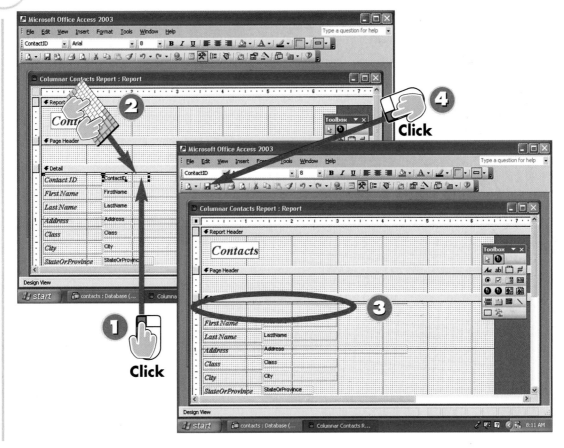

Click

Click

1. After you open in Design view the report that contains the field you want to delete, click the field's text box control to select both the label *and* the text box.

2. Press the **Delete** key on your keyboard.

3. The field is deleted.

4. Click the **Save** button on the Standard toolbar in the main Access window to save the change to the report.

End

Suppose that you want your report to include only certain fields from the selected table. In that case, you can easily delete from the report any fields you don't need.

Was Only the Label Deleted?

If only the label was deleted, you did not select the text box. You must select the text box to delete both the label and the text box

Undoing the Deletion

If you change your mind, you can undo the deletion by clicking the **Undo** button on the Standard toolbar in the main Access window or by opening the **Edit** menu and choosing **Undo**.

Resizing a Report Control

Start

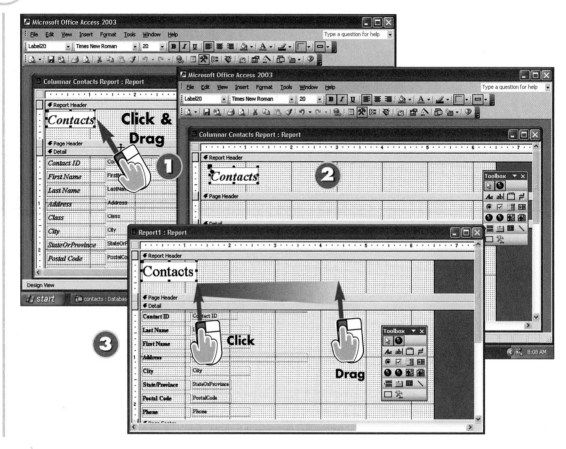

(1) To change the size of a report section, place the mouse pointer on the section's border, click, and drag.

(2) The report section is resized.

(3) To resize a label, click it to select it, and then drag one of the sizing handles (any black box except for the bigger box in the upper-left corner) until the label is the size you want.

TIP

Using the Big Selection Handle
The bigger box you see when you select a control is used for moving the control. See the next task for information on moving.

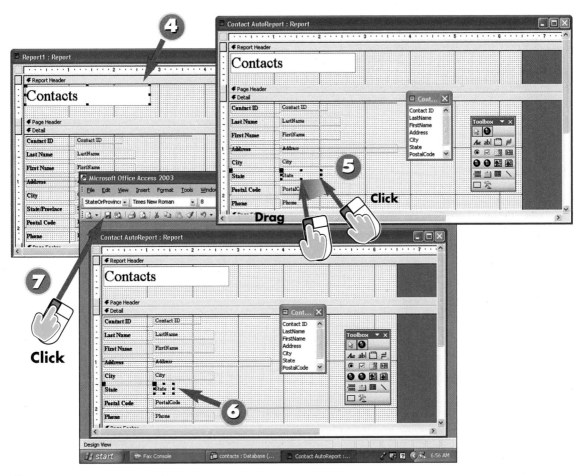

4 The label is resized (here, made larger).

5 To resize a text field, click it to select it, and then drag one of the sizing handles (any black box except for the bigger box in the upper-left corner) until the text field is the size you want.

6 The text field control is resized (here, made smaller).

7 Click the **Save** button on the Standard toolbar in the main Access window to save the change to the report.

End

No Automatic Adjustments
Access does not make an automatic adjustment if one control overlaps another. You need to manually move and resize the controls so that they don't overlap.

Resizing the Report
You can also resize the report itself, making it larger to make more room, for instance. To resize, put the pointer on the report border and drag to resize.

Moving a Report Control

Start

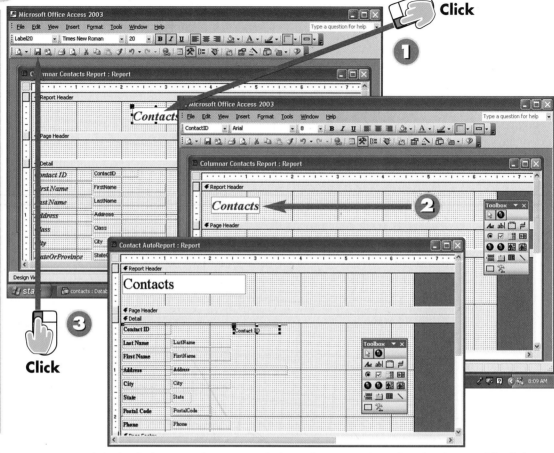

Click

1 To move a label, click it to select it, and drag the move handle (the larger black box) in the upper-left corner.

2 The label is moved.

3 To move just the text box, select it, and then drag the move handle in the upper-left corner of the text box (not the label). Just the text box is moved. Click the **Save** button.

End

One change you might want to make to your report is to rearrange the order of the fields it contains. For example, you might want to move a label away from its text box to provide more space between the two. You can move a label, the text box, or both the label and text box.

TIP

Moving a Label and Text Field
To move both the label and the text field, click the text field to select both controls. Click within the label (not on the move box) and drag the fields to a new location. Notice that both the label and the text box are moved.

Adding a Field to a Report

Start

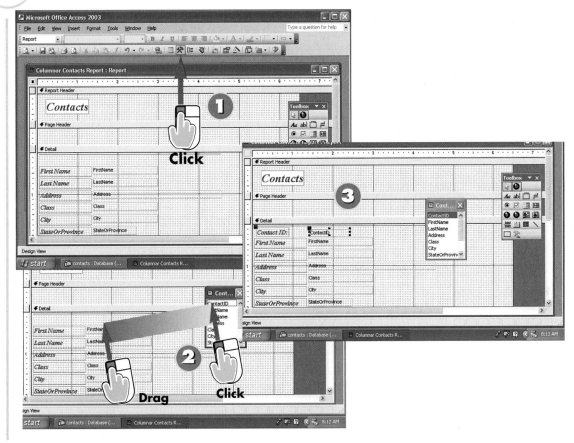

1. After you open in Design view the report to which you want to add a field, click the **Field List** button on the Standard toolbar in the main Access window.

2. A list of fields in the current table appears. Click the field you want to add to select it, and drag it to the location on the report where you want it to be placed.

3. Access adds a label and text box for the field. (You may have to make some adjustments to the size and placement.)

End

INTRODUCTION

When you create a report with a wizard, you select which fields are included. If needed, however, you can add more fields to the report. You can even add fields from other tables.

TIP

Resizing Sections
You may need to resize the section in which the new field is placed to make room for the new field. To do so, place the mouse pointer on the section's divider line or border and drag it.

TIP

Displaying the Field List
If necessary, you can open the **View** menu and choose **Field List** to display the list. To close the list, click its **Close** button.

Adding Labels to a Report

Start

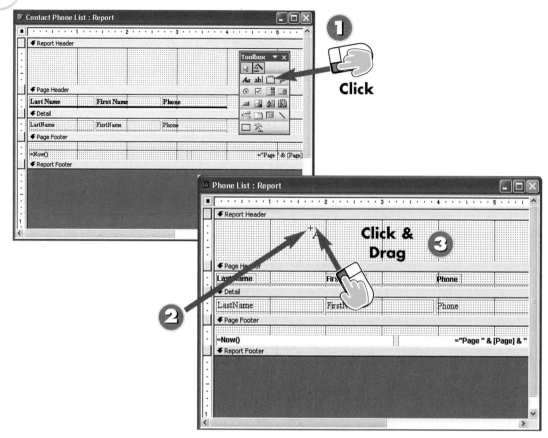

Click

Click & Drag

1. After you've opened the report you want to modify in Design view, click the **Label** button in the Control toolbox.

2. The mouse pointer becomes a plus sign with a capital A. Move the pointer to the spot in the report where you want to create the label.

3. Click and drag to draw the text box for the label.

If the information in a report is not self-explanatory, it's a good idea to add other identifying information, such as a descriptive report title, the author's name, the company name, and other items. To do so, you simply add a text box control to the report and include the necessary information in the control.

TIP

Placement

Keep in mind that the placement of the label affects where it appears in the report. If you place the label in the page header, it appears at the top of every page. If you include the label in the Details section, it is included with the detailed information for each record in the report.

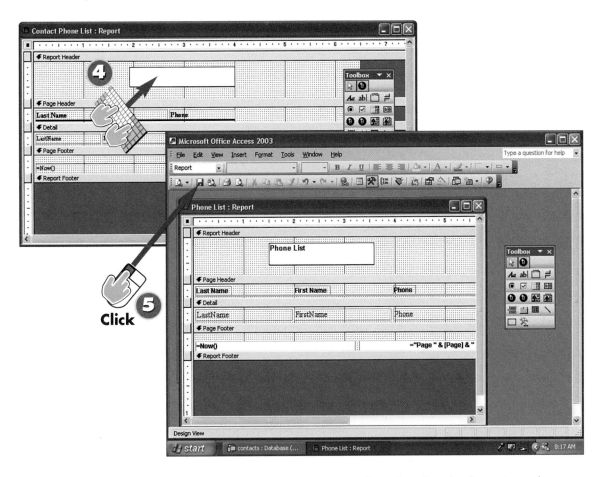

4 The text box is added, and the insertion point is placed within the box. Type the label text.

5 The label is added. Click the **Save** button on the Standard toolbar in the main Access window to save the report.

End

Editing a Label
You can edit a label by clicking in the label's text box. You can then edit the text as needed or select all the text, press **Delete**, and type new text.

Formatting Label Text
You can format the text in the label much like formatting text in a Word document. To do so, select the text box and then use the formatting buttons in the toolbar or the commands in the Format menu.

Adding Headers or Footers to a Report

Start

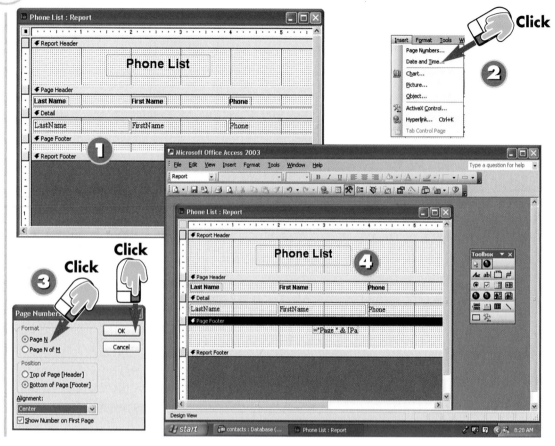

① To resize a header, place the mouse pointer on the header section divider line, click, and drag.

② The header section is resized. To add page numbers to a header or footer, first click in the header or footer. Then open the **Insert** menu and choose **Page Numbers**.

③ The Page Numbers dialog box opens. Select the desired **Format**, **Position**, and **Alignment** options, and click **OK**.

④ Page numbers are added to the header or footer. To add the date or time, click in the desired header or footer, open the **Insert** menu and choose **Date and Time**.

INTRODUCTION

You might want to include identifying labels on headers and footers because the page headers and footers print on every page. In addition to adding identifying labels, you can add other objects—such as page numbers—to the header or footer. Before you add items to your headers and footers, you may need to resize the header or footer section first. If you used AutoReport or the Report Wizard to create your report, headers and footers may already be added (you can delete them if you don't want them).

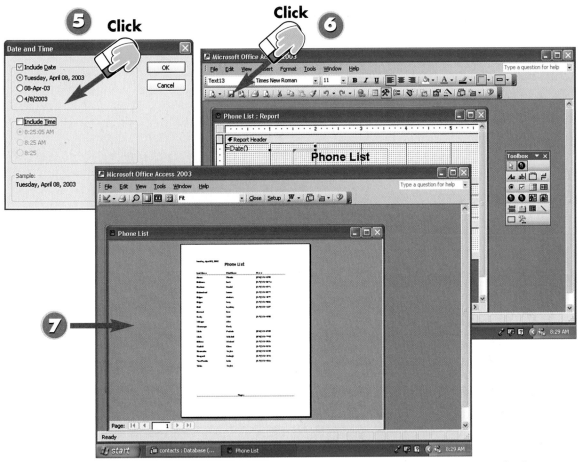

5 The Date and Time dialog box opens. Click the **Include Date** and/or **Include Time** check boxes to select them, and specify how the date/time should appear. Click **OK**.

6 The date/time is added to the header or footer you selected (here, to the Report header). Click the **Save** button on the Standard toolbar to save the report design.

7 To view the changes as they will appear when printed, preview the report. (For help previewing your report, see the task "Previewing a Report" later in this part.)

End

Deleting the Header or Footer Object
To delete a header or footer object, click it to select it and then press the Delete key on your keyboard.

Adding Text
You can also add text to the header/footer, such as the company name, by adding a new label and placing it within the appropriate header or footer section. Refer to the task "Adding Labels to a Report" earlier in this part for more information.

Adding a Logo
As another option, you can add a picture to your report. If you want the logo to print on all pages, insert it in the Page Header or Page Footer section. To print the logo on only the first page, insert it in the Report Header section.

Drawing on a Report

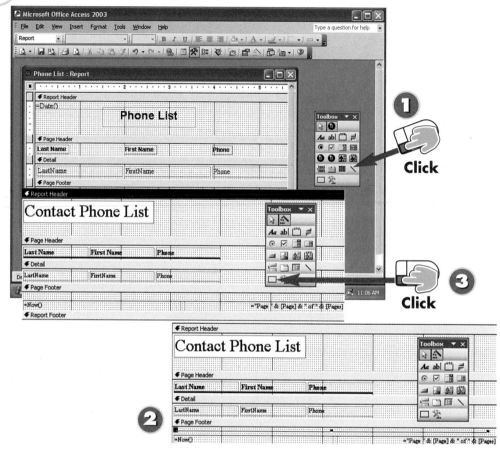

1 After you open the report you want to modify in Design view, click the **Line** button in the Control toolbox.

2 Move the mouse pointer to the area on the report where you want to draw the line, click, and drag. When the line is the desired length, release the mouse button; the line is added.

3 To draw a rectangle, click the **Rectangle** button in the Control toolbox.

INTRODUCTION

In addition to adding text and fields, you can also include graphical elements in your reports using certain tools in the Control toolbox. One such tool is the Line tool, which you can use to draw a line to separate columns or to separate the report title from the report. Alternatively, you can use the Rectangle tool to draw a box around a label to add emphasis.

**Click &
Drag**

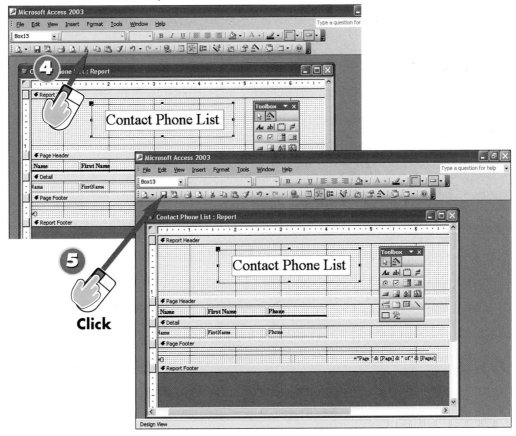

Click

4 Move the mouse pointer to the area on the report where you want to draw the rectangle, click, and drag. When the box is the desired size, release the mouse button; the box is added.

5 Click the **Save** button on the Standard toolbar in the main Access window to save the report.

Straight Line, Perfect Square
To draw a straight line or perfect square, hold down the **Shift** key as you drag.

Using the Undo Command
To get rid of a line or box you've added to your report, open the **Edit** menu and choose **Undo** immediately after you add it. Alternatively, click the line or box to select it and then press the **Delete** key on your keyboard.

Using Other Tools
You can use the other tools in the Control toolbox to draw and create more sophisticated reports and forms. For more information about all the various Control toolbox tools, refer to Access's online help.

Adding a Picture to a Report

Start

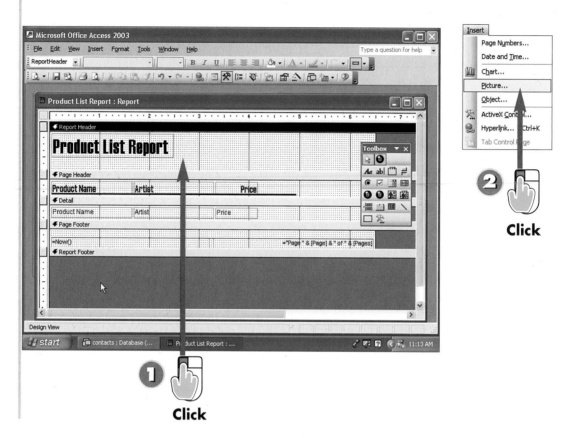

Click

Click

1 After you open the report you want to modify in Design view, click in the section in which you want to insert a picture.

2 Open the **Insert** menu and choose **Picture**.

In addition to data, labels, and drawn objects, you can also include a picture in your report. For example, you might include your company logo, an illustration, or a figure. You most often add a picture to one of the headers, but you can also insert pictures in other sections of the report.

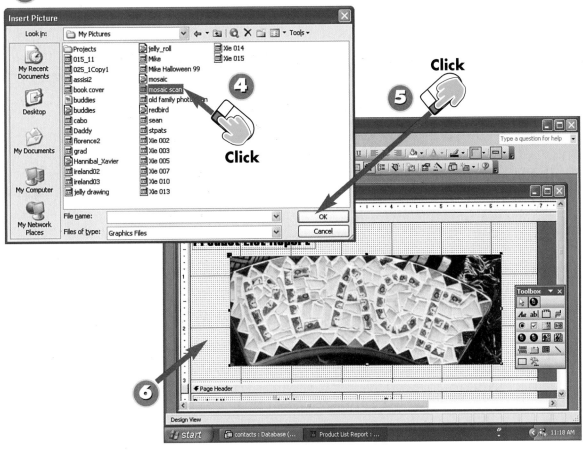

The Insert Picture dialog box opens. Using the Look in drop-down list or the Places bar, locate and open the folder that contains the picture file you want to add to your report.

Click the picture you want to insert to select it.

Click **OK**.

The picture is inserted. (You may need to move or resize the picture.)

End

Moving, Resizing, and Deleting

You move or delete pictures just like you do any other report object. First select it and then drag to move it or press the **Delete** key to delete it.

Sorting and Grouping Data in a Report

Start

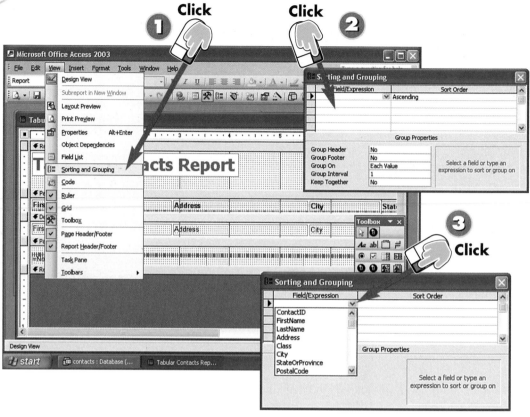

Click 1

Click 2

Click 3

1. After you open the report whose contents you want to sort or group in Design view, open the **View** menu and choose **Sorting and Grouping**.

2. The Sorting and Grouping dialog box opens. Click the first cell in the **Field/Expression** column; a down arrow appears.

3. Click the **down arrow** in the **Field/Expression** column and select the field on which you want to group. For example, to group by state, select the **State** field.

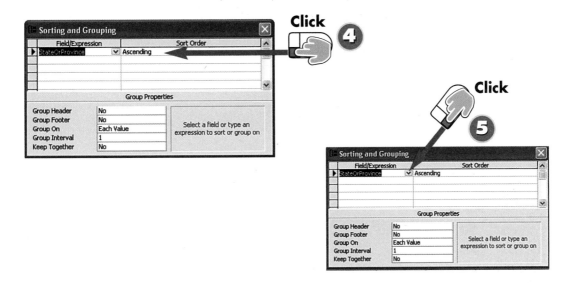

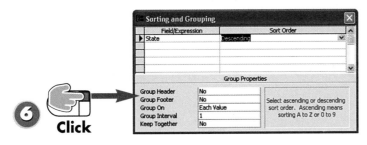

Click 4

Click 5

6 **Click**

4 The default sort order is ascending. If you prefer to sort in descending order, click the first cell in the Sort Order column. Then click the down arrow that appears.

5 Click the **down arrow** in the **Sort Order** column and choose **Descending** from the list that appears.

6 If you want to display a header (or footer) for each group, click either the **Group Header** or **Group Footer** field; a down arrow appears.

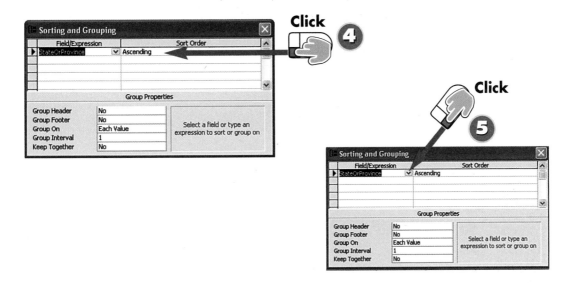

See next page

Group Headings

The report will be grouped in order, but the order might not be apparent unless you add a group header as well as a label to identify that group. For example, if you grouped by state, you could add the state field (not the label) so that at the start of each new state you would see the state in the group header.

Sorting and Grouping Data in a Report (Continued)

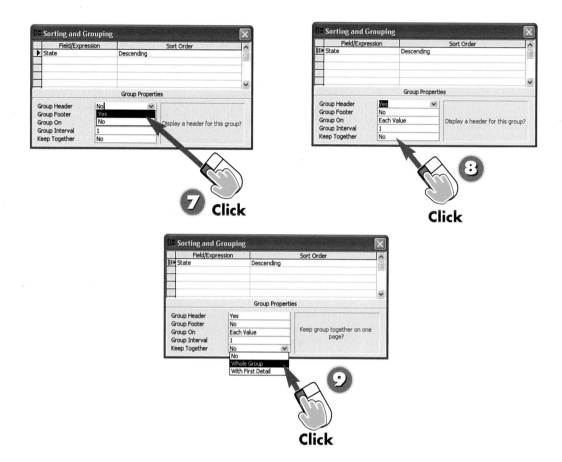

7 Click

8 Click

9 Click

7 Click the **down arrow** that appears in either the **Group Header** or **Group Footer** field and choose **Yes** from the list that appears.

8 If you want to keep the entire group together (that is, with no page breaks), click the **Keep Together** field; a down arrow appears.

9 Click the **down arrow** in the **Keep Together** field and choose an option for keeping the fields together: Whole Group or With First Detail.

Setting Other Properties
You can change other properties of the group. For example, use the Group On property to select the value or range of values that starts a new group.

TIP

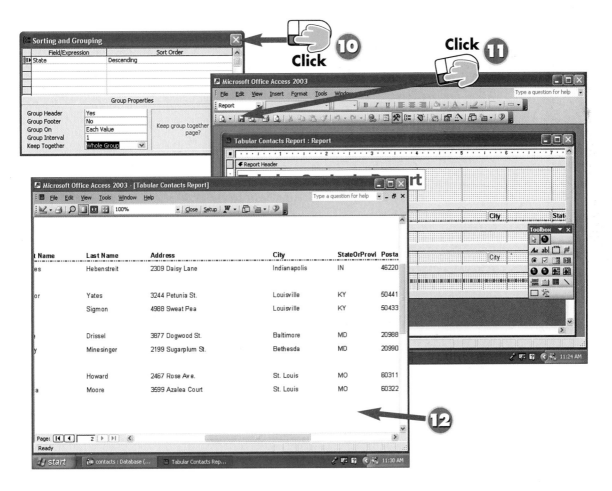

Click **10**

Click **11**

10 Click the Sorting and Grouping dialog box's **Close** button to close it.

11 You see the report design, including new header/footer sections if you added a group header/footer. Click the **Save** button on the Standard toolbar to save the report design.

12 To see the results of the grouping, preview the report. (For more information about previewing, see the task "Previewing a Report" later in this part.)

End

Using Expressions

This example uses a simple group, but you can create more complex groups by using *expressions*. For example, you can group products by price (all products less than $50, $50–$100, $100 or higher, and so on). Part 6 provides some information about using expressions to group data; you can also consult Access's online help for more information.

Using a Report AutoFormat

Start

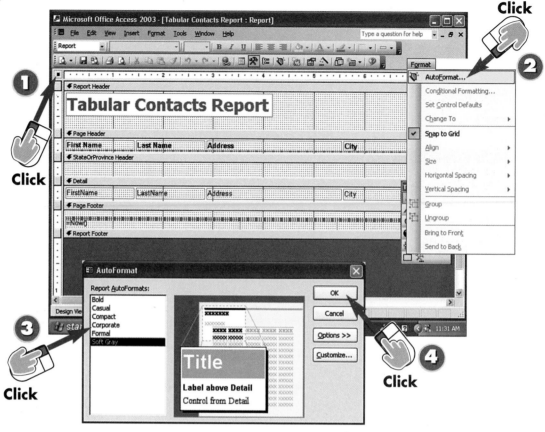

1 Click in the upper-left corner of the report to select the entire report.

2 Open the **Format** menu and choose **AutoFormat**.

3 The AutoFormat dialog box opens containing a list of the available formats. Click a format.

4 A preview of the selected format appears on the right-hand side of the dialog box. If this is the format you want to use, click **OK**. (Otherwise, repeat step 3.)

INTRODUCTION

If you want a quick way to change the appearance of your report without making individual modifications to the sections, objects, and so on, you can use an **AutoFormat**. This applies a coordinated set of formatting choices.

TIP

Selecting AutoFormat Options
You can select which options from the AutoFormat are applied by clicking the **Options** button in the AutoFormat dialog box. In the dialog box that appears, uncheck any of the options you don't want to use (font, color, or border).

Click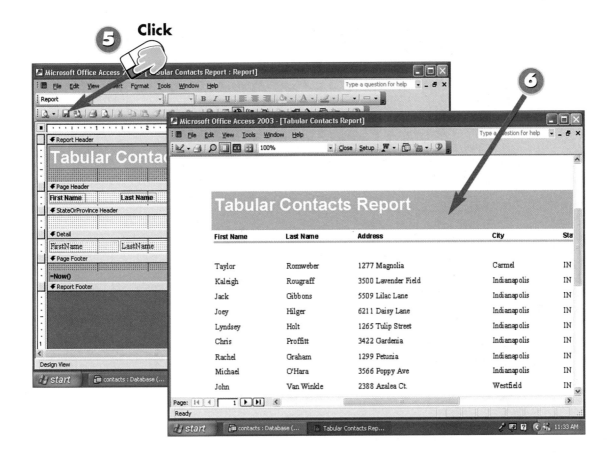

5️⃣ Access applies the selected AutoFormat to your report. Click the **Save** button on the Standard toolbar in the main Access window to save the report.

6️⃣ To see how the report will look with the AutoFormat applied, preview the report. (For information about previewing, see the task "Previewing a Report" later in this part.)

End

TIP

Formatting Individual Objects
You can also format each individual control, label, text box, section, and other report parts. To do so, double-click the object you want to change. A dialog box containing the formatting options for the selected object appears.

TIP

Customizing a Report
If you make additional formatting changes to your report after applying the AutoFormat and want to include them in the AutoFormat itself, click the **Customize** button in the AutoFormat dialog box. You can then select to create a new AutoFormat, update the existing AutoFormat, or delete the AutoFormat.

Setting Up the Page

Start

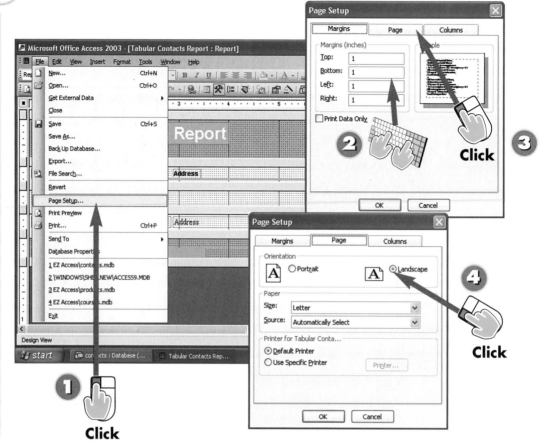

Click

1 After you open the report you want to modify, open the **File** menu and choose **Page Setup**.

2 The Page Setup dialog box opens. In the Margins tab, change any of the margin settings: Top, Bottom, Left, and Right. (The default value is 1.)

3 To change page options, click the **Page** tab.

4 Select an orientation for the report. If the report contains only a few fields, choose the **Portrait** option; otherwise, choose **Landscape**.

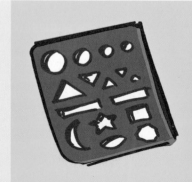

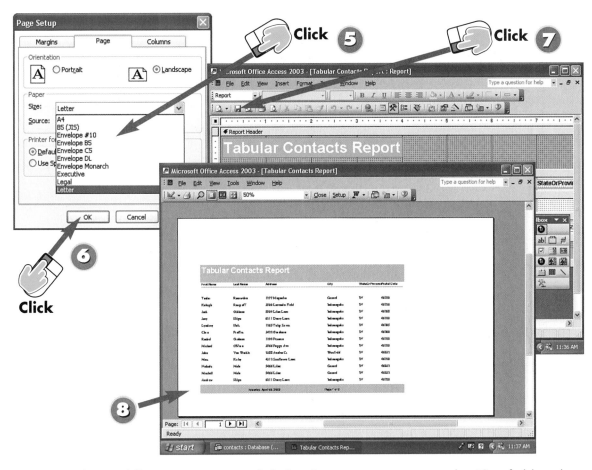

5. To select a different paper size, click the **down arrow** next to the **Size** field and select a size from the list that appears. (Your printer must be able to handle the selected paper size.)

6. Click **OK**.

7. Access returns you to Design view. Click the **Save** button on the Standard toolbar in the main Access window to save the changes to the report's design.

8. To see how the page-setup options affect the report, preview it. The preview shown here shows a different top margin, landscape orientation, and legal size paper.

End

Columnar Reports
For columnar-style reports, you can click the Columns tab and make changes to the number of columns, the size of the row spacing and columns, and the way in which the columns flow (down and then across or across and then down).

Previewing a Report
For information about previewing reports, see the next task.

Previewing a Report

Start

Click **2**

Click

1

Click **3**

Click

4

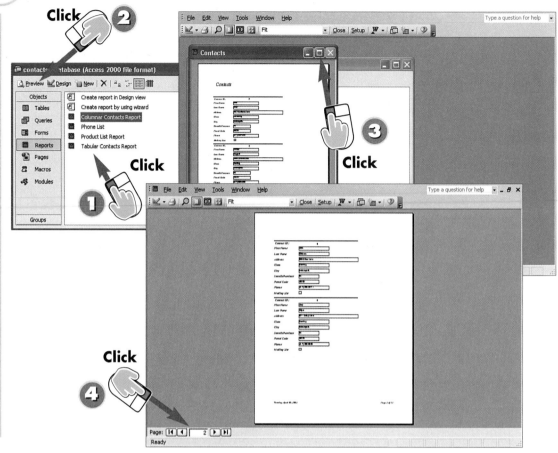

1 In the database window, click the report you want to preview to select it.

2 Click the **Preview** button.

3 The report is displayed onscreen. If necessary, maximize the window by clicking its **Maximize** button.

4 Click the **Page** buttons to move to other pages in the report.

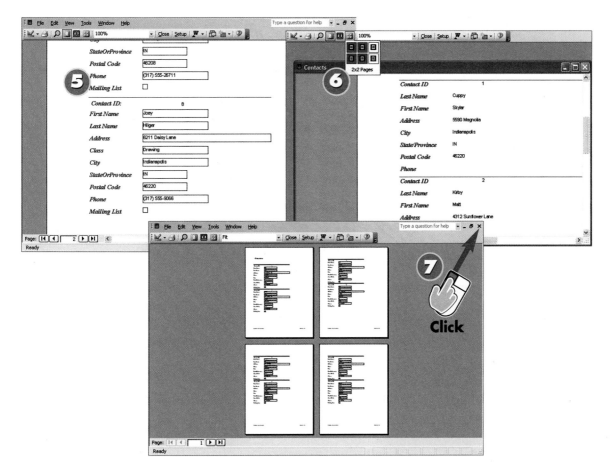

Click

5 To zoom in, click the area of the report you want to view. Access zooms in on the area you clicked. To zoom back out, click anywhere in the preview.

6 To view multiple pages side-by-side, click the **Two Pages** or **Multiple Pages** button. If you click **Multiple Pages**, drag across the palette to select the number of pages to display.

7 You see several pages displayed at once. Click the **Close** button to close the report.

End

Zooming In
You can also open the **View** menu and choose **Zoom** to zoom in (or out) by a certain percentage.

Using Design Layout View
Another view option is Design Layout view. When you are working in Design view, you can switch back and forth between Design view and Layout Preview as you work.

Choosing Print, Design, or Setup
You can print directly from the preview by clicking the **Print** button. To access the page setup options for the report, click the **Setup** button in the preview window.

Printing a Report

Start

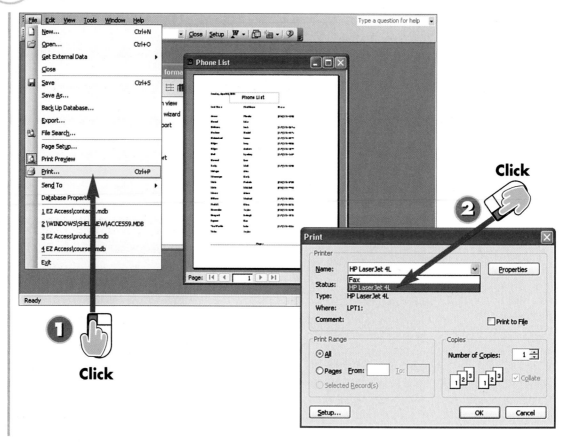

Click

Click

1 After you open the report you want to print, open the **File** menu and choose **Print**.

2 The Print dialog box opens. To select a printer other than the default, click the **down arrow** next to the **Name** field and select a printer from the list that appears.

Most reports are created with the purpose of printing them. After you have created and formatted your report, set up the page, and checked its appearance by previewing it, you are ready to print.

TIP

Previewing First
Because you can't really get a good idea of how the report will look from within Design view, it's a good idea to preview the report first. Make any necessary modifications, preview again, and then print.

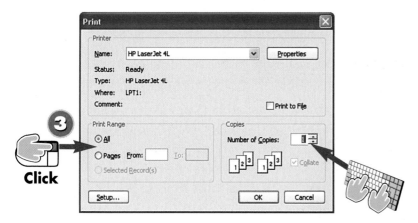

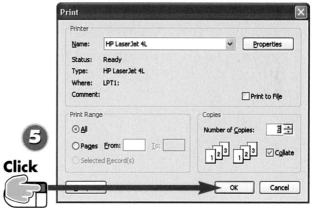

Click

Click

3 In the **Print Range** area, specify the pages in the report that you want to print (the default setting is **All**) .

4 To print more than one copy of the report, type the number of copies you want in the **Number of Copies** field.

5 Click **OK**. The report is printed.

End

Printing Multiple Copies

If you select to print multiple copies of your report, you can opt to collate the pages by marking the **Collate** check box. If you uncheck this check box, Access will print the set number of copies of page 1, followed by the set number of copies of page 2, and so on.

Managing Your Database

Now that you have learned how to create many different types of database objects, including forms, queries, tables, reports, and the like, it's time to step back and look at the database as a whole. This part covers common tasks you'll need to perform to maintain your database, including renaming an object, deleting an object, and securing your data with a password.

In addition, this part covers setting up relationships among the tables in your database. Access is a relational database and rather than include one huge table, you'll find it better to create several smaller, more focused tables, and then link or relate the tables together as needed. Using various tables, you can create queries, forms, and reports that pull data from several of these tables.

table relationship

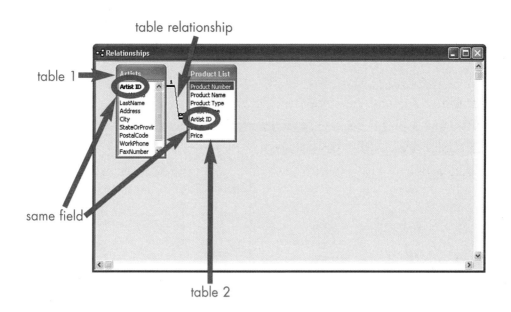

table 1

same field

table 2

Renaming an Object

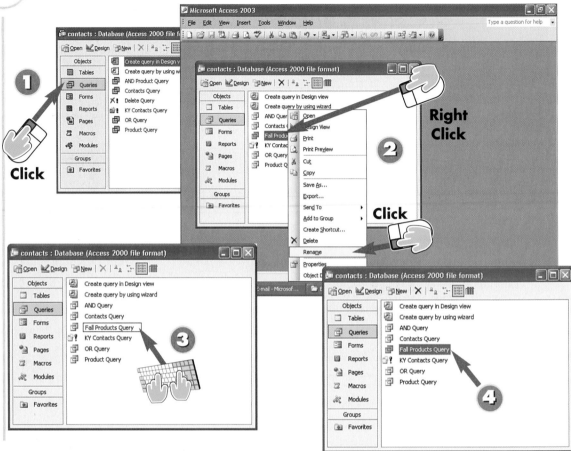

1 After you've opened the database that contains the object you want to rename, click the object type in the Objects bar. For example, to rename a query, click **Queries**.

2 The database window displays a list of the objects of that type. Right-click the object you want to rename and select **Rename** in the shortcut menu that appears.

3 The name is highlighted. Type a new name for the object and press **Enter**.

4 The object is renamed.

If you do not like the name you used when you saved an object, you can rename it. You may find, for instance, that you want to use the word "**Query**" in the names for queries, "**Report**" in the names for reports, and so on; that way, you can quickly identify the object type without having to check the Objects bar.

Using Other Commands
You can use the other commands in the shortcut menu to copy the object, view object properties, print the object, and more.

Deleting an Object

Start

Start

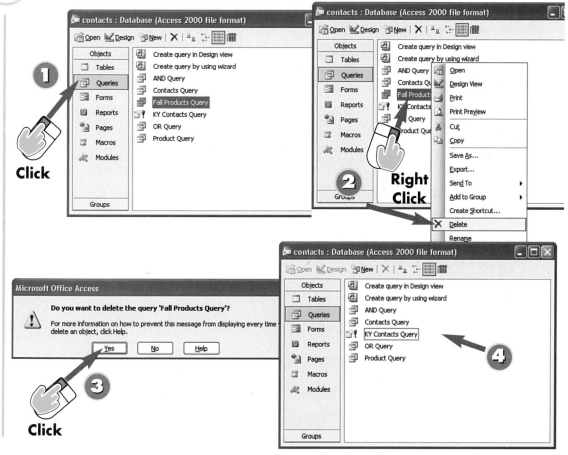

1 Click

2 Right Click

3 Click

4

1 After you've opened the database that contains the object you want to delete, click the object type in the Objects bar. For example, to delete a query, click **Queries**.

2 The database window displays a list of the objects of that type. Right-click the object you want to delete and select **Delete** in the shortcut menu that appears.

3 Access prompts you to confirm the deletion. Click **Yes**.

4 The object is deleted.

End

INTRODUCTION

If you no longer need an object, you can delete it. Suppose that you created a query for practice and now want to delete it so that it is not listed in the database window or saved as part of the database. Keep in mind that if you delete a table, you are also deleting all the data in that table.

TIP

No Undo
You cannot undo an object deletion, so be sure this is what you intend. If you do not want to delete the object, click **No** when prompted in step 3.

TIP

Clicking Delete
If you prefer, you can click the object you want to delete to select it and then click the **Delete** button in the database window's toolbar.

Password-Protecting a Database

Start

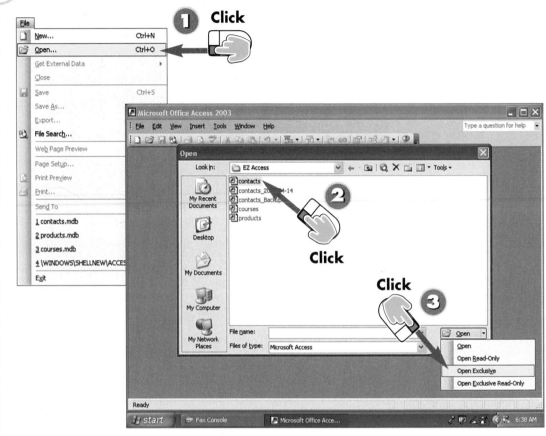

Click ①

Click ②

Click ③

---

① Open the **File** menu and choose **Open** to display the Open dialog box.

② Using the **Look in** drop-down list or the **Places** bar, open the folder that contains the database you want to open and click the database to select it.

③ Click the **down arrow** next to the **Open** button and choose **Open Exclusive** from the list of options that appear.

INTRODUCTION

Chances are, more than one person uses your database. For this reason, you might want to assign a password to that database so that only users with the password can access it. To assign a password, you first must use a special procedure for opening the database, as outlined here.

Other Security Features

TIP

Access provides many more security features, including features for setting up user and group permissions for editing (if several individuals use the database) and encrypting the database contents. For more information, consult Access's online help.

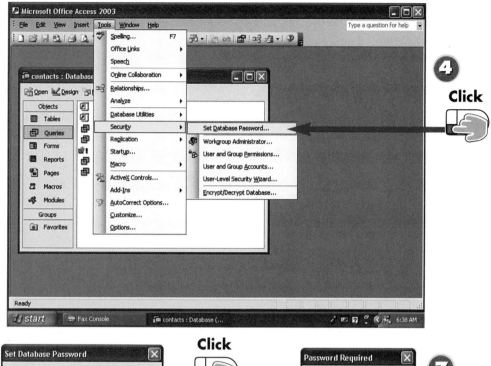

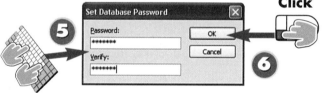

Click

4 The database opens; you can now assign a password. To begin, open the **Tools** menu, choose **Security**, and select **Set Database Password**.

5 In the **Password** field, type the password you want to assign. Then, press **Tab**, and retype the password in the **Verify** field.

6 Click **OK**. Access returns you to the database window.

7 If you close and then try to reopen the database, Access prompts you to type the password. Type the password and click **OK**.

End

Not Opened Exclusively?
If you do not open the database exclusively, you'll see an error message when you attempt to apply a password. Clear the error message, close the database, and follow steps 1–3 to open the database again.

Dropping the Password
To get rid of the password you've assigned, open the database. Then, open the **Tools** menu, choose **Security**, and select **Unset Database Password**. Type the password in the dialog box that appears and click **OK**.

Backing Up the Database

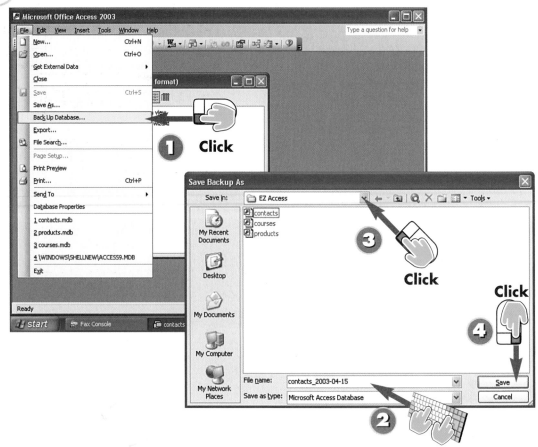

(1) With the database you want to back up displayed onscreen, open the **File** menu and choose **Back Up Database**.

(2) The Save Back Up As dialog box opens, with a suggested name for the backup file in the **File name** field. If you want, select the suggested name or type over it with a name you prefer.

(3) Using the **Save in** drop-down list or the **Places** bar, open the folder in which you want to store the backup file.

(4) Click the **Save** button. A backup copy of your database is created.

End

If anything bad happens to your database file, all your data could be lost. That's why it's important to back up your data, and to do so frequently. When you back up your database, you create a separate file that contains the data in your database.

Viewing Your Backup File
You can view your backup file by opening the **File** menu and choosing **Open**. Then, open the folder that contains your database backup file, click the file to select it, and click the **Open** button.

Tape Backup
If you have many databases or large databases, consider checking out some of the other backup tools and programs available. For example, you might want to use a *tape backup drive*, which speeds the backup process.

Viewing Database Properties

Start

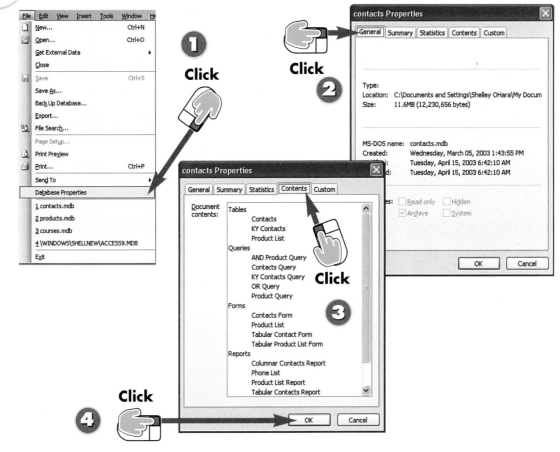

Click ❶

Click ❷

Click ❸

Click ❹

❶ With the database whose properties you want to view displayed onscreen, open the **File** menu and choose **Database Properties**.

❷ The database's Properties dialog box opens. To view general file information, click the **General** tab.

❸ Click any other tab to view more information about the database. For example, to see a list of all the objects in the database, click the **Contents** tab.

❹ Click **OK** to close the Properties dialog box.

End

If you want to view information about your database file, you can display its properties. The Properties dialog box lists information about the size of the file, key dates (that is, the dates the file was created, modified, and accessed), and other data, such as the contents of the database.

TIP

Viewing Database Statistics
The Statistics tab lists the dates that the database was created, modified, accessed, and printed. It also lists the last person who saved the file, the revision number, and the total editing time.

Setting Up Relationships

Start

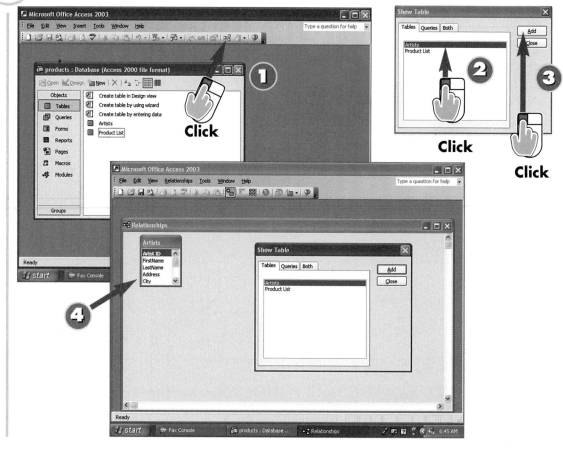

Click

Click

Click

1 With the database for which you want to establish relationships displayed onscreen, click the **Relationships** button on the Standard toolbar in the main Access window.

2 The Show Table dialog box opens with the Tables tab displayed. Click the first table for which you want to establish a relationship to select it.

3 Click the **Add** button.

4 A window representing the table you added (here, **Artists**) is displayed onscreen. To link another table to the one displayed, click it in the Show Table dialog box.

INTRODUCTION

It's much easier to manage a database when you work with several tables rather than one huge file. For example, suppose that you sell products and use Access to track orders, product lists, inventory, and clients. If you stored all that information in one database table, the table would be difficult to work with. If, though, you create tables for each specific task or action and then set up relationships, you'd be able to work with data more easily. For example, you could link the Orders table to the Product table to pull product information. You could also link the Client Information table to the Orders table so that you could access client information as part of the order. To create these types of links, you set up relationships between tables.

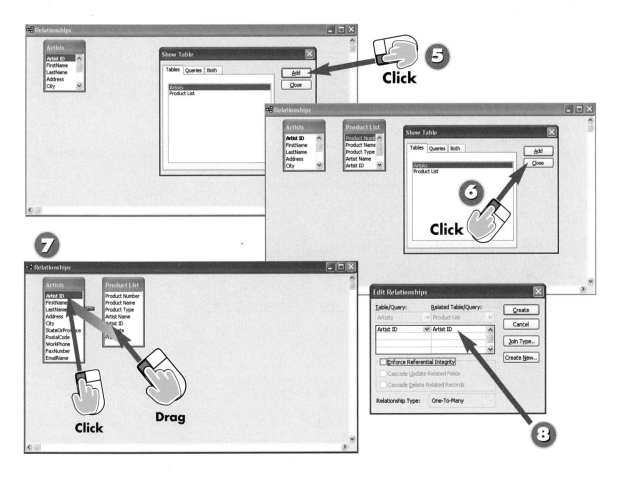

5 Click the **Add** button.

6 A window representing the second table you added (here, **Product List**) is displayed onscreen. Click the **Close** button in the Show Tables dialog box to close it.

7 In the first table window, click the field you want to use to establish a relationship (here, **Artist ID**) and drag it to its matching field in the second table window.

8 The Edit Relationships dialog box opens; in it, you can set options on how the relationship you've established will work. Make sure that the correct fields are listed as the linked fields.

See next page

Sharing Fields
To set up relationships between tables, the tables must share one field in common. Usually this is some type of unique ID field. The field does not have to have the same name but must contain the same data type and data.

Resizing the Table Window
If necessary, resize the table windows to better view all the fields each one contains. To do so, put the pointer on the border of the field list and drag.

Removing a Table
If you add a table to the Relationships window by mistake, you can remove it from the window by right-clicking the table window and choosing **Hide Table** from the shortcut menu that appears.

Setting Up Relationships (Continued)

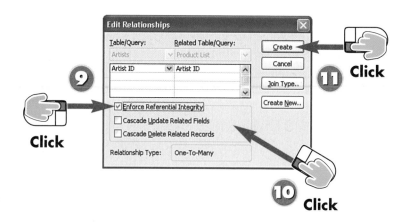

9 If you want to enforce referential integrity, click the **Enforce Referential Integrity** check box to select it.

10 The **Cascade Update Related Fields** and **Cascade Delete Related Records** check boxes become available; if desired, mark one or both check boxes.

11 Click the **Create** button.

Understanding Referential Integrity

When you turn on referential integrity, Access keeps the related tables in sync. That means if you mark the **Cascade Update Related Fields** check box and make a change to the related field in one database table, the change will also be made in the related database table. Likewise, if you mark the **Cascade Deleted Related Records** check box and delete a record in one table, any associated records in the related table are deleted as well.

Click

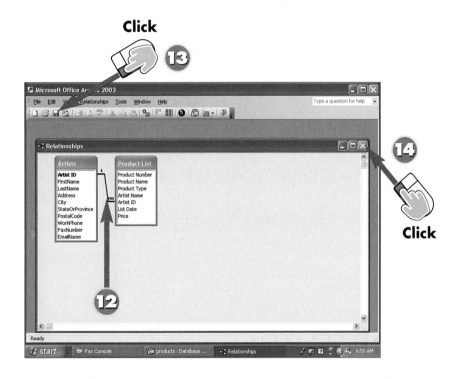

Click

Access establishes the relationship. A line links the two related fields in the Relationships window. (If you enabled referential integrity, the line indicates this with a chain link symbol.)

13 Click the **Save** button to save the relationship.

14 Click the **Close** button in the Relationships window to close it.

End

Editing Relationships

Start

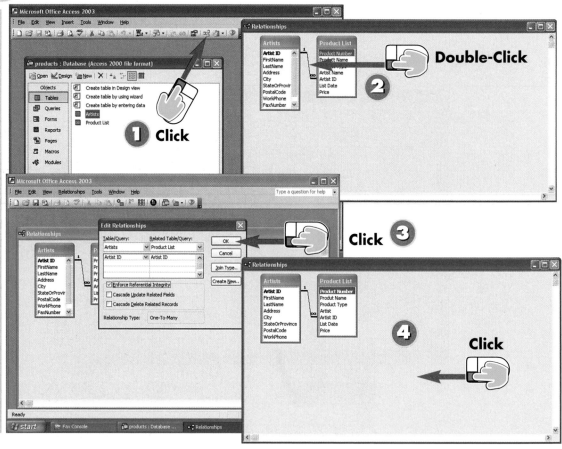

Double-Click

Click ③

Click ④

Click ①

① With the database whose relationships you want to edit displayed onscreen, click the **Relationships** button on the Standard toolbar in the main Access window.

② To change the relationship options, double-click the relationship line.

③ The Edit Relationships dialog box opens. Make changes as needed and click **OK**.

④ Click the **Save** button on the Standard toolbar in the main Access window to sav the changes.

End

After you have established a relationship between tables, you may need to make changes. For example, you might decide to change the options for how the relationship works, or you might want to delete the relationship.

TIP

Deleting Relationships
To delete a relationship, click the relationship line to select it and press the **Delete** key on your keyboard.

Using Subdatasheets

Start

Click ①   **Click** ②

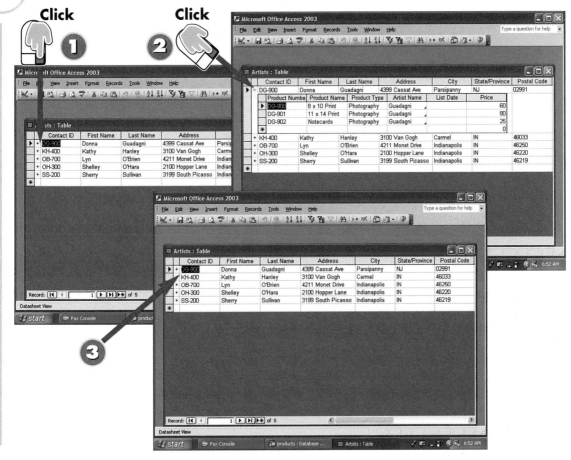

① After you've opened the first database table, click the **plus sign** next to the record whose subdatasheet you want to view.

② The data from the related table is displayed. To hide the subdatasheet, click the **minus sign** next to the record.

③ The subdatasheet is hidden.

End

You might want to view (and possibly change) data in a table that is related to another table. To do this, you display the first table's *subdatasheet*. The subdatasheet displays the record information from that related table. You can then collapse (hide) or expand (show) the related record in the other table.

Editing the Subdatasheet
You can edit data in the subdatasheet. If you have set up the relationship to enforce referential integrity, the changes will be made and saved in the original, related table.

A

AutoForm   A type of form that uses default values to create a simple form for data entry.

AutoFormat   A predesigned set of formatting options that you can use with forms and reports to quickly change that object's appearance. AutoFormat options may include different fonts, background colors, and other formatting changes.

AutoNumber field   A type of field that is automatically entered and incremented. If you do not set the primary key, but ask Access to do so, it creates an AutoNumber field and uses this field as the primary key. AutoNumber fields are useful if you need to keep track of the order in which records were entered.

AutoReport   A type of report that uses a default layout to create a simple report.

C

control   Items on a form or report that help create the structure and layout of the form or report. For instance, a label control on a form could identify the field name. In addition to labels, a control can also display data from the database table. For instance, in a typical form, you see the label and the data for that field, both of which are created by controls.

Currency field   A type of field used when you want to enter monetary amounts.

D

data format   A predesigned layout for the display of data in a field. You can select, for instance, the format in which dates and times are displayed.

data type   A property of a field that specifies the kind of data stored in that field.

database   A program, such as Access, used for entering, viewing, editing, and manipulating data.

Database template   A predesigned database that contains tables, reports, queries, and other database objects designed for specific purposes such as a contacts database.

database window   The window that appears when you open a database; this window lists all the available types of objects as well as commands for creating new objects.

datasheet   A tablelike grid of rows and columns used for entering data into a table.

Date/Time field   A field used for storing dates and times.

Design grid   The lower half of the Query Design window. You use this grid to enter the criteria for your query.

F

field   An individual piece of data. In Access, you start with a table, and that table contains fields. You can include as many or as few fields as needed. A field has a unique field name, a data type, and a field size. You can also set other elements for the field.

field caption   Text that you can add to a field that will be used for the field label (rather than the field name) in a form.

field description   Text that is displayed when that field is selected. You can use a field description to aid in data entry.

field property   An option that you can set for a field to control how the field appears or works. For instance, you can set the Required property to Yes to require an entry in a particular field.

field size   The size of the field; different field types have different default sizes. You can change the size as needed.

filter   A method for displaying only a subset of records. You can filter records in a table, form, or query.

filter expression   Similar to an equation; you can create an expression for comparing and then filtering data— for instance, all products that cost more than $100 (>100).

form   A method for entering data into the data table. Rather than a large grid that displays many records, you can display and enter data one record at a time.

H–I

hyperlink field   A type of field used for storing email addresses, Web site addresses, or links to documents.

input mask   A preformatted setup that helps the user enter data in the proper format. For instance, a phone number input mask might look like this: (___) ___-____

L–M

label   The text that identifies a field in a form or report. You can also add unbound labels (not attached to a particular field). For instance, you could add a report title or a header or footer, as unbound labels.

macros   An Access object that can automate a task. This book does not cover creating macros.

Memo field   A type of field that enables you to store long entries of text. This type of field is useful for notes, for instance.

N

navigation buttons   The buttons that appear along the bottom of a datasheet or form that enable you to move from record to record.

Number field   A type of field used for storing numbers.

##

objects   The various items that you can create in Access. Objects include tables, forms, reports, queries, macros, and pages.

Objects bar   In the database window, the area that lists the types of available database objects. Click the type of object to access commands to create a new object of that type or to open or modify an existing object.

OLE Object field   A type of field used to store another type of document, such as a picture, worksheet, Word document, and so on.

P

pages   A type of Access object used for displaying and accessing Web-formatted data.

primary key   A field in a table that uniquely identifies each record. For instance, a table's primary key may be a field that holds each recorded person's Social Security number.

Q–R

query   A type of Access object that enables you to retrieve specific information that meets the criteria you enter. For instance, you could create a query to list all customers that live in South Carolina. Or you might create a query that lists all students that received an A in English.

record   A set of related fields. For instance, in a contact database, the name, address, phone numbers for, say, John Doe would be one record.

record selector   The first column in a list of fields or records. You can click this field to select a record.

relational database   A type of database program that enables you to store information in one or more tables and then relate those tables to create a cohesive information system. Access is a relational database program.

relationship   The link between two (or more) tables. Some relationships are one-to-many. For instance, suppose that you had a student table and a courses table. Each student could take more than one course. Thus, this type of relationship is a one-to-many. In a one-to-one relationship, each record relates to only one other record. For instance, if you had a courses table and a professor table, each individual course would relate to only one individual professor.

report   An Access object that enables you to print a summary of data from a table or query.

S

Smart Tag   An assignment to certain types of entries (such as names) that enable you to perform common tasks. For instance, if names Smart Tags are on, you can send an email and perform other tasks at any place that name appears.

sort   To rearrange the records in a database table in alphabetical or numerical order, ascending or descending.

subdatasheet   Another database table that has a relationship with the current table. You can display and enter and edit records in the subdatasheet.

switchboard   If you use a template to create a database, a switchboard is created. You can use this list of tasks rather than the database window to create, open, and edit database objects.

T

table   The main type of object in Access. A table stores your data and is comprised of fields, each with a unique name (see *field*). One set of related fields is a record (see *record*).

template   A predesigned database that already includes tables, forms, reports, and other object types. You can use a template to quickly create a database. Access includes several common database templates.

Text field   The most common type of Access field, this field stores (as its name implies) text. Keep in mind that some text fields can contain text, numbers, or a combination. For instance, a phone number is best stored as a text field because you aren't likely to perform numerical calculations on that field.

W-Z

wizard   An Access feature that helps you build an object such as a table, form, or report. You make your selections, clicking Next to move from screen to screen, to create the new object.

Yes/No field   A type of field that can store one of two entries: yes or no (or on/off, true/false).

T